DOING BUSINESS IN 21ST CENTURY INDIA

DOING BUSINESS IN 21ST CENTURY INDIA

HOW TO PROFIT TODAY IN TOMORROW'S MOST EXCITING MARKET

GUNJAN BAGLA

**BUSINESS
PLUS**

NEW YORK   BOSTON

Business Plus
Hachette Book Group USA
237 Park Avenue
New York, NY 10017
Visit our Web site at www.HachetteBookGroupUSA.com.

Business Plus is an imprint of Grand Central Publishing.
The Business Plus name and logo are trademarks of Hachette Book Group
USA, Inc.

Printed in the United States of America

First Edition: July 2008

10 9 8 7 6 5 4 3 2 1

Library of Congress Control Number: 2008920233
ISBN-10: 0-446-40224-9
ISBN-13: 978-0-446-40224-8

Book design by Charles Sutherland

CONTENTS

INTRODUCTION

Why You Need This Book Now

Whether you're an executive, a manager, an investor, or a small-business owner, you likely know that the second fastest-growing market in the world is India—and that a piece of the tremendous opportunity that exists there could be yours. That's why you picked up this book.

Is India right for you and your company? Or would you be just following the crowd?

As a native of India and a management consultant to top Western businesses on this very subject, I caution clients about the challenges involved in engaging with this region. Pitfalls are plentiful, and profitability could elude you for a decade or more if you are not careful about picking the right opportunities. Located halfway around the world from North America, India may require a flight of more than fifteen hours (if you are lucky enough to live near an airport that offers nonstop service). Many supposedly adventurous executives hesitate to relocate their families to India, and even global giants such as Apple Computer and Starbucks Coffee have announced, then shelved or delayed, plans for India.

It is easy to come to the wrong conclusion when you start to engage with India. It's a complicated, confusing place. With two dozen languages and a billion people, this is the world's biggest and most fractious democracy. State governments change regularly, mind-numbing lists of regulations flourish and multiply, and the cacophonous traffic could drive even a seasoned Bostonian crazy. There are no magic formulas or simple solutions to success in a country that American ambassador and Indophile John Kenneth Galbraith once described as a "functioning anarchy."

On the other hand, for every company that has retreated from India, there's one that has had a go at it—and some have reaped great rewards. Take IBM. When it was included among the NASSCOM trade association's top twenty information technology and software services exporters in June 2004, IBM asked to be removed from this list. Friends inside the company told me that the company feared a possible backlash, due to the offshoring of American jobs, on Main Street and even on Capitol Hill.

But just two years later, IBM changed its tack dramatically. For the first time in its history, IBM held its annual stock analysts' meeting outside the United States—in India! Fifty top stock analysts from the likes of Deutsche Bank, Goldman Sachs, JPMorgan, Lehman Brothers, and Morgan Stanley flew halfway around the world to report on this pep rally for IBM investors. *BusinessWeek* compared it to a rock concert. And indeed it was a memorable event in June 2006, when IBM's CEO Sam Palmisano stepped in front of eleven thousand people under a giant air-conditioned blue tent in the city of Bangalore to announce that the company was about to invest $6 billion in India over the next three years, tripling its original $2 billion outlay over the previous three years. With forty-three thousand IBMers in fourteen of its cities, India was host to IBM's largest country organization outside the United States. (As of December 2007, one out of five IBMers is based in India, with a total of seventy-three thousand employees in-country.)

There was no mistake about it: Palmisano and his IBM team had made the momentous and strategic decision to tie the firm's future to India. Now they *wanted* the world to take notice.

IBM's dramatic expansion of its Indian operations helped change the way corporate America looks at India as a market, as a resource, and as a long-term strategic opportunity. In later chapters, we will look at General Electric, Citibank, PepsiCo, and others that also led the way.

This book will equip you with the knowledge and skills to ask the right questions about business in India and listen to surprising answers with an open mind. I've written it from the point of view of a practitioner rather than an academic or a researcher. Reading it won't make you an India expert. In fact, parts of India's business scene are changing so rapidly that few can claim to be experts for long. However, with the aid of input from seasoned top business people in the region—both Western and native—I will show you how to become an India *student,* and I will give you the tools to identify and pursue top business opportunities in this emerging market.

One of the most essential (and encouraging) things to understand about India is that contrary to many outsiders' expectations, its secrets are not hidden behind an arcane culture, a complex language, or citizens who won't talk to you. On the contrary, India is an incredibly open society. For example, many senior government officials list their home addresses and phone numbers on their business cards. Unlike many of its Asian neighbors, India enjoys a domestic press that is one of the most free, expressive, and competitive in the world. And Indians have ready access to most media from the West. Still, India can be hard to understand, because it emits a thousand conflicting signals to the new visitor. Two smart, well-traveled Americans can witness the same business situation and come away with dramatically different conclusions. It happens all the time, and keeps my California-based management consulting practice quite busy.

But before we delve into more of what Westerners are doing in India, let's take a look at the story of the Ambani family, who exemplify the unique nature of business in modern India.

If the name *Ambani* sounds familiar to you, it's probably because the Ambani brothers are the heirs to the largest private-sector company in India, called Reliance. Mukesh Ambani is ranked fifth on *Forbes* magazine's 2008 list of the world's billionaires. And his brother Anil is right behind at number six. (He holds vast interests in the telecom, power, and entertainment industries.) As you might guess, there's a great story behind this filial rivalry. In fact, neither Hollywood nor its Indian cousin, Bollywood, could have soaped up a melodrama like the one that had India spellbound for seven months starting in fall 2004.

But first, a bit of important background.

Born to modest means in 1932, Anil and Mukesh's father, Dhirubhai Ambani, dropped out of school and worked as a dispatch clerk in what is now Yemen, at a time when most of India's large domestic private companies were run by men born to wealth. (Think Andrew Carnegie, who spent his early teens as a telegraph messenger in Pittsburgh eighty years before.) As in most rags-to-riches stories, few could have predicted that this son of a schoolteacher would one day control a $15 billion empire. Indeed, Ambani was India's most remarkable businessman. Ever.

Ambani rose from being a spice trader to the founder and CEO of Reliance Textile Industries Ltd. When he took his company public on the Bombay Stock Exchange in 1977, he convinced millions of middle-class Indians to buy stock (in Reliance, of course) for the first time. And while corporate India chafed in the 1980s under the government bureaucracy known as License Raj, which constrained private-sector companies' production capacity, Ambani insisted that he was deaf to the word *no*. As a result, Reliance grew exponentially, and so did its number of stockholders. By 2002, original investors in Reliance's initial public offering had earned an incredible 43 percent per year compounded annual rate of return, and Reliance became the first Indian private-sector company to enter the Fortune Global 500.

That same year, Dhirubhai Ambani died without leaving a will. Elder son Mukesh was promptly elected company chairman, but rumors of discontent between his brother Anil and him began circulating in the press. Anil had allied himself with a north Indian political party, earning him a seat in India's upper house of Parliament—which many viewed as a direct challenge to his brother. Reports of friction abounded, and in November 2004 Mukesh Ambani finally confirmed that there were significant problems between the two.

This public admission put the three million Reliance stockholders on edge, which, in turn, made the company's customers, vendors, employees, and even government officials nervous. The media fed this anxiety as each brother and his camp began leaking stories about the other. Concerned banker friends, cabinet ministers, family members, and board members all visited the Ambani mansion to resolve the differences, to no avail. Months went by, with daily headlines from the contentious camps. Rumors, accusations, and worse swirled. Most people assumed Reliance's best days were behind it.

In March 2005, there was a breakthrough of sorts—and not the kind you'd expect.

Astrologer Yogesh Aillawadi made a prediction in the *Times of India,* India's largest circulating English-language newspaper: "Both brothers would become successful and [their company] Reliance will do better in future times to come." He blamed the planet Mars for all the brothers' troubles, and said they would resolve their differences by spring.

Three months later, as if on cue, the prophecy was fulfilled. Kokilabhen Ambani, Dhirubhai's widow and the brothers' mother, declared an "amicable" split of the Reliance fortune between Mukesh and Anil. According to *The Economist,* "This [announcement] followed late-night talks driven by Mrs. Ambani on the advice of religious astrologers consulted by the group on the timing of all decisions." That day, the Sensex—India's version of the Dow Jones Industrial Average—soared to a record high as Indians celebrated the power of motherhood and astrology to resolve disputes.

The lesson? No matter what the century, no matter how big the business, *never* underestimate the power of family—and of religion and astrology—in Indian business. I am not suggesting that you start basing your decisions on your horoscope or visiting palm readers. But keep in mind that your Indian customer, vendor, partner, or government official might do so, and I promise that you will begin to understand what makes the new India tick by the time you have completed reading this book.

In 2006, Morgan Stanley Research declared China and India to be the "new tigers of Asia." Yet as someone who grew up in India and has spent his adult life in California, I think the more apt characterization is an elephant. An elephant is more complex, more friendly, and more intriguing than a tiger. I'm not the first to make this comparison.

When Vermont poet John Godfrey Saxe (1816–1887) scribed these verses inspired by an ancient fable from India ("Indostan," as he called it), he might well have been describing modern American executives dealing with India.

The Blind Men and the Elephant

It was six men of Indostan
  To learning much inclined,
Who went to see the Elephant
  (Though all of them were blind),
That each by observation
  Might satisfy his mind

The first approached the Elephant,
  And happening to fall
Against his broad and sturdy side,
  At once began to bawl:
"God bless me! but the Elephant
  Is very like a wall!"

The second, feeling of the tusk,
  Cried, "Ho! what have we here
So very round and smooth and sharp?
  To me 'tis mighty clear
This wonder of an Elephant,
  Is very like a spear!"

The third approached the animal,
  And happening to take
The squirming trunk within his hands,
  Thus boldly up and spake:
"I see," quoth he, "the Elephant
  Is very like a snake!"

The fourth reached out an eager hand,
  And felt about the knee.
"What most this wondrous beast is like
  Is mighty plain," quoth he;
"'Tis clear enough the Elephant
  Is very like a tree!"

The fifth, who chanced to touch the ear,
  Said: "E'en the blindest man
Can tell what this resembles most;
  Deny the fact who can
This marvel of an Elephant
  Is very like a fan!"

The sixth no sooner had begun
  About the beast to grope,
Than, seizing on the swinging tail
  That fell within his scope,
"I see," quoth he, "the Elephant
  Is very like a rope!"

And so these men of Indostan
  Disputed loud and long,
Each in his own opinion
  Exceeding stiff and strong,
Though each was partly in the right,
  And all were in the wrong!

Is India poor or rich, old or new, fast or slow, vast or small, powerful or weak? Does it celebrate religious diversity? Or does it condemn minorities? Can illiterate people support democracy? How can you have a free press in a country where millions of people are starving? You can visit India like the blind men and see just one answer to these and other questions, or you can read this book and begin to see the full picture.

If there's one thing I've learned from my twenty years of consulting on the subject, there's no single road map to success in India. Instead, I've tried to give you the next best thing: sound advice, inside knowledge, and important background, all drawn from the insights of many accomplished Western expatriates in the region, as well as from my own experience. It won't put me out of business, but it will give you the best shot at plotting your course and discovering your own piece of business in India and its many rewards.

CHAPTER 1

The Big Opportunities

For the astute and prudent company, India today can be a gold mine. There is money to be made in the most unexpected places, if you look carefully and plan right. While major risks and significant pitfalls surely exist, a self-assured India now welcomes Western executives to its free market on fair terms in a vibrant and complex democracy.

Much of American media would have you believe that business in India equates to outsourcing and American job loss. Call centers near Delhi and computer programmers in Bangalore continue to be the staple of many news stories. But that's only a fraction of global business based in India that we hear about. Western companies that successfully sell products and services in India seldom receive equal press coverage. For example, it's been little reported that General Electric sold $3 billion of goods and services in India in 2006 and has publicly stated that its goal is $8 billion by 2010.

Let's take a look at some current mega-trends— manufacturing, defense, infrastructure, consumer goods, and finally knowledge-based services—as well as some emerging trends that show signs of taking off in the near future.

Manufacturing

Every year, the Union of Japanese Scientists and Engineers selects a few companies for its prestigious Deming Application Prize for quality, named after the famous American management consultant who helped transform Japanese companies with the principles of statistical quality control. Until 1997, not a single factory in India had ever won a Deming, which has been called the Nobel Prize of manufacturing. Just nine years later, sixteen Indian companies, mostly in the automotive business, had won Deming awards, including Rane Brake, Sundaram Clayton, the seat division of Krishna Maruti, Rane Engine Valves, Rane TRW Steering Systems, Brakes India, and TVS Motors. That's more winners than *any* country outside Japan.

Ten years ago, most of the industrial world did not regard India as a manufacturing powerhouse, but since then a number of remarkable accomplishments have made the nation one of the world's top destinations for manufacturing.

Here's a quick survey: $58 billion Korean carmaker Hyundai established a presence in India in 1996 and is now the country's second largest. A few years later, Hyundai began exporting cars made in Chennai, India, to markets in Europe, Africa, the Middle East, and Latin America. In 2008, Hyundai plans to export three hundred thousand cars from India.

India is one of the few countries that features homegrown automotive companies. Tata Motors gained the world's attention at the 2008 Delhi Auto Show, when it showed the world's least expensive car the Nano, but it has been selling the Indica, a hatchback, followed by the Indigo, a sedan, for several years. All three models were designed entirely by Tata. Mahindra and Mahindra, whom we will also meet later on in the book, produces a sports utility vehicle called the Scorpio.

At the same time, spurred by strong domestic markets and smart management, automotive suppliers in India began improving their quality and productivity. Batteries, radiators, alternators, and other automotive components made in India are routinely exported to North America. Recently, I was invited to visit the world's largest single-location metal-forging facility, located in Pune about 120 miles from Mumbai. I was surprised and impressed to tour the factory, owned by Bharat Forge Ltd. Robotic assembly lines start with steel billets at one end and finish with completed crankshafts for cars and trucks ready to load onto pallets at the other, without any routine human intervention.

India's manufacturing transformation is not limited to the automobile industry. Overall industrial production rose by 12.5 percent in fiscal year 2007 compared with the previous year. In the global pharmaceutical industry, it is not easy to receive manufacturing approval from the US Food and Drug Administration (FDA). Yet India now boasts seventy-five FDA-approved facilities, more than any country outside the United States; Italy is next with fifty-five FDA-approved facilities, and China is third with twenty-seven.

If you want to understand the future of India, you should know about the city of Jamnagar, in western India. In 2000, the world's third largest refinery, with a capacity of 660,000 barrels per day, began operations here. American companies such as Bechtel provided construction expertise. Others, including General Electric, Foxboro, and Rockwell Automation, provided equipment. Owned and operated by India's largest private-sector company, Reliance Industries Ltd., the Jamnagar complex was built in less than three years and has won numerous industry awards in its six years of operations; it was named the most energy-efficient refinery in 2004 by Shell Global Solutions, and Refiner of the Year in 2005 by Hart Energy Publishing. A port and a power plant were built specifically to support the refinery.

Reliance is now building the world's sixth largest refinery, a $6.1 billion plant next to its existing refinery. California-based Chevron Corporation decided to invest $300 million in return for 5 percent ownership. At this new refinery, ExxonMobil's research and engineering unit provided the technology for the world's largest sulfuric acid alkylation plant. Much of the new refinery's product is meant for export to Europe and the United States. When the 580,000-barrel-per-day refinery is completed at about the time this book goes to press, it will make Jamnagar the world's largest petroleum-refining hub.

You should also know about hundred-year-old Tata Steel, which recently transformed itself to become the lowest-cost producer of steel on the planet. World Steel Dynamics ranked it the best steelmaker in 2005 and 2006—and soon it will be one of the biggest. Not only is Tata's principal Indian facility—located in Jamshedpur, and with a capacity of five million tons per year—undergoing a significant expansion, but three new locations are also being planned in the Indian states of Jharkhand, Orissa, and Chhattisgarh, with capacities of twelve, six, and five million tons per year, respectively. In a later chapter, we will look at Tata Steel's remarkable overseas acquisitions.

There are other signs of strength in manufacturing in India from diverse sources. The world's second largest producer of blank CDs and DVDs, Moser Baer, is located near New Delhi. If the manhole covers in your city are imported, chances are good that they were manufactured at a foundry in India. Swiss engineering giant ABB Group is in the midst of a $200 million expansion in India. Its president of global markets, Ravi Uppal, summed it up when he told *BusinessWeek* in October 2007, "Manufacturing is where India's future lies; this is the real economy."

The boom in manufacturing in India brings about three types of opportunities. First of all, if your company supplies any products, equipment, or services to manufacturers, you may find a very ready market in India. Second, if you want to benefit from India's manufacturing prowess, you may find a good vendor partner. Third, your company may benefit from setting up its own facilities in-country.

Defense

India has the world's largest military that depends primarily on imported equipment. More than 1.1 million people serve in its all-volunteer armed services, and the country spends over 2.5 percent of its GDP on defense. The vast majority of its current installed base of hardware was purchased from the former Soviet Union, with some armaments provided by British, French, and Swedish entities.

But the future may not be like the past; in fact, it could be radically different.

In the wake of President George W. Bush's war on terror, India and the United States see each other as allies fighting the same immediate enemy. Military planners in India view their strategic interests spanning the Indian Ocean littoral from Africa to the Straits of Malacca; they want its aircraft to be able to reach Central Asia and its ballistic missiles to be a threat to more than just Pakistan.

Fifty thousand vessels a year pass through the Straits of Malacca, south of Singapore, making up one-quarter of all oceanic trade worldwide. At one point, the navigable channel is just a few miles wide. The Nicobar Islands, six hundred miles east of Chennai in the Bay of Bengal, are part of India and offer an excellent potential choke point for this trade. Some people refer to the island of Car Nicobar as India's stationary aircraft carrier, standing sentinel over these vital lanes. Economic growth and increased trade make India eager to defend shipping lanes from the

Persian Gulf toward East Asia. In this, the United States and India are aligned.

Perhaps driven by frustrations that former Soviet vendors are now spread across Russia, Ukraine, Georgia, and other countries, and perhaps by a desire to align more closely with geopolitical realities, the Indian government has broadened its sourcing plans.

The best evidence of this is Israel. India and Israel did not even have full diplomatic relations until 1992. By 2006, however, Israel had leapt into place as India's second largest military supplier, and India has become Israel's largest customer of defense products and services.

The United States has made some progress in winning defense contracts as well. India ordered about $150 million of Raytheon Corporation weapons-locating radars in 2002, and purchased the former USS *Trenton* warship from the US Navy for $48 million in 2006. In September 2007, when the country released its largest-ever request for proposals—126 modern aircraft—both the Boeing Company and Lockheed Martin Corporation were invited to bid on the $10.5 billion program. In the near future, India plans to buy field artillery guns, airborne early warning systems, long-range maritime surveillance aircraft, several kinds of helicopters, and unmanned aerial vehicles (UAVs). It plans to spend $30 to $50 billion on defense purchases in the coming decade. Western companies can bid freely for most of these contracts. Will there be substantial wins? No one knows for sure. But it's a huge new opening.

Infrastructure

To many visitors, India's infrastructure in the twenty-first century looks like it was transplanted from the nineteenth century. On city streets, you might see cows, camels, donkeys, mules, horses, and an occasional elephant competing with automobile traffic. In rural areas, paved roads are a luxury. Local trains in Mumbai run overfull and don't even have doors for safety. Electric power plants are inadequate and outdated; they suffer high failure rates. Power to homes, offices, and factories continues to be unreliable across the country. Educated people hesitate to drink the municipal water unless it is boiled or filtered first. A growing population and a booming economy only add stress to the creaky infrastructure.

You could complain about these challenges and give up on India. Or you could look upon each of them as a business opportunity. Let's look at some recent examples.

When India decided to build a world-class metro train system in the capital, Delhi, one of the five consulting companies hired for the massive project was Parsons Brinckerhoff (PB) of New York. The first phase of the train system was completed and operational well ahead of schedule. Delhi's trains are air-conditioned and sleek, its stations are modern, and the system is transforming the way many people work and live. After seven years as an expatriate, John Triplett, who led Parsons India before becoming an independent consultant, believes the country has a great future. "I think that US companies, with the proper attitude and direction, can be very successful here. When I arrived in India, many people thought that Parsons Brinckerhoff was British." PB is now well known and respected in India as a US company.

A thirty-year contract to improve, operate, and manage Delhi Airport was awarded in January 2006 to a public–private partnership (PPP) that includes Germany's Fraport, for its operations expertise, and Malaysia's Eraman for its background in airport retailing. Each has 10 percent, whereas India's GMR Infrastructure Ltd. controls just over half. The government of India controls about a quarter through the Airport Authority of India. When completed, the airport will have the capacity to handle a hundred million passengers a year. In southern India, Hyderabad's brand-new airport, with a starting capacity of twelve million passengers, is also a PPP owned by GMR. Malaysia's Airports Holding Berhad is an 11 percent partner. The ultimate annual capacity of this airport might be forty million passengers. Mumbai's airport is the busiest in India. It was privatized and handed over to a similar PPP led by GVK Industries Ltd. of India, which includes two overseas partners from South Africa, conglomerate Bidvest Group, and state-owned Airports Company, SA. In addition to the minority foreign investors in the PPPs, dozens of additional overseas vendors stand to gain as they sell the hundreds of millions of dollars of imported products and services that will be required to develop and operate these and other airports.

While several American companies have shied away from infrastructure opportunities in India, more than twenty-eight hundred employees of the Bechtel Corporation, with headquarters in San Francisco, have been working on the engineering, procurement, project management, and construction consulting for the $6 billion expansion to Reliance's refinery in Jamnagar in western India since January 2005.

Chances to participate in improving India's infrastructure will increase over time. It's seldom easy to win business deals that involve any government. It is even harder when the victory involves an Indian joint-venture partner that holds a majority stake. However, in the next decade, the railways, highways, bridges, seaports, power plants, and refineries of India will need hundreds of billions of dollars of upgrades to keep up with economic progress. Western firms can hardly afford to sit out the dance.

Consumer Goods

On July 24, 2006, a new character entered the world of Archie Comics. Raj Patel was featured in a story called "Out-raj-eous Behavior." In case you have forgotten, Archie and his friends Betty, Veronica, Jughead, and Reggie are students at the fictional Riverdale High School. The small New York company that publishes the comics is run by the sons of two of the original founders. While the comics might be past their prime in the West, they are immensely popular among Indian middle-class schoolchildren. The debut of Raj Patel was front-page news—because he is Indian.

Penguin India, publisher of J. K. Rowling's *Harry Potter and the Deathly Hallows,* reported more than 252,000 advance orders for the new title in 2007. Tent-pole Hollywood movies are often released at the same time in India and are being dubbed into local languages. American media giants including MTV, CNN, Google, Yahoo!, and MSN are all popular in India.

The Western media in all its forms influences and shapes Indian middle-class opinions and expectations. The Washington, DC–based Pew Research Center found in successive surveys (2002, 2005, and 2006) that most Indians have a positive view of the United States. In Russia and China, two other large markets with economic growth potential, most citizens view America negatively according to Pew's 2006 findings. Many American companies have an opportunity to leverage this attitude into business.

A growing population, rising per-capita income, and an expanding middle class have created a "perfect storm" of increasing demand for almost every type of consumer product or service imaginable. Whether your company sells consumables, durables, or services, few locations will let you grow your top line to the extent that you can in India over the next decade. We will explore this further in chapter 5, "Marketing in India."

Knowledge-Based Services

If your company has any work that is to be performed using a computer or a telephone for Western customers or for in-house use, chances are you might benefit by having some of that work performed in India. The correct term for this process is *offshoring*.

You may have this work performed by a subsidiary of your own company. Citibank, Texas Instruments, and General Electric were among the earliest American companies to recognize how to profit from such an Indian operation. More commonly, such work is sent to a vendor with operations in India; this is properly called *offshore outsourcing*. In some cases, your outsourcing vendor is a Western company that has an Indian back end, such as Accenture, IBM, EDS, Cognizant, ACS, CSC, Hewlett-Packard, or the like. In other situations, you may find it expedient to use an Indian vendor directly. India's largest offshore outsourcing vendors are Tata Consultancy Services, Infosys, Wipro, Satyam, and HCL. Hundreds of smaller Indian vendors thrive today, most by specializing in an industry, such as banking, video games, or pharmaceuticals, or in a function like customer contact, data analytics, quality assurance, or accounts payable. In common parlance, all such initiatives are lumped under the catchall of *outsourcing*.

An alphabet soup of acronyms describes these processes further, including information technology outsourcing (ITO), business process outsourcing (BPO), knowledge process outsourcing (KPO), legal process outsourcing (LPO), transcription outsourcing (TO), contract research outsourcing (CRO), information technology enabled services (ITES) . . . and the list goes on.

It is a mistake to think that this opportunity is only about labor arbitrage. In fact, the initial impetus for the information technology outsourcing business in India came about because there simply weren't enough programmers in the

West to cope with correcting software systems to meet Y2K requirements. The lower cost was gravy.

"Selecting a vendor is no longer about simply finding the best price. Western clients now look at the vendor's focus area," says Arjun Malhotra—who founded one of India's top IT companies, Hindustan Computers Ltd., and built its US operations to $100 million in annual revenues in the 1990s. "They also look for companies that can add value to the business issues that are of central concern to their own company's needs." Malhotra now runs Headstrong, Inc., in Fairfax, Virgina, an IT and management consultancy.

Today, smart Western companies continue to use India for knowledge work to save money and expand capacity. But the *really* smart ones are those who also leverage resources in India to reduce time to market, to increase the rate at which new products can be launched, to free their onshore staff for more critical projects, and to be able to address Asian and third-world markets. In short, they use India as a strategic advantage against their competitors.

This is not painless, of course. Globalizing knowledge-based work has its pitfalls—and we will examine several of them in this book. But those companies that figure out how to do it well have become addicted to globalization. That is why direct employment in this field in India continues to grow at more than 20 percent per year. The best-run companies are growing in India at faster than 30 percent per year as of this writing.

Real Estate

Property prices in urban areas rose rapidly between 2004 and 2007. While subject to short-term hiccups, property is generally a good investment for Indians. Indian developers have been very successful in raising capital on domestic markets.

According to Karun Verma, the Bangalore-based local director of real estate services firm Jones Lang LaSalle Meghraj, India is different from other markets at this time because commercial real estate generally leads retail and residential development. Each square foot of commercial construction is followed by two to three square feet of retail and eventually seven to ten square feet of residential construction.

Verma states, "While construction, building sales, and tenancy practices are all at world levels in India, land acquisition continues to be a hazy process." Foreign companies can buy land and build for their own use, but cannot speculate in real estate. Many foreign companies prefer to lease rather than buy. India still limits foreign investment in real estate, although rules were relaxed somewhat in 2005.

As of this writing, foreign investors can only invest in "greenfield" projects with minimum thresholds sometimes in excess of one hundred thousand square yards; there are several other rules as well. Most American investment interest has come from private-equity firms such as Starwood Capital Group and Walton Street Capital, both of which announced participation in a billion-dollar, twenty-million-square-foot township in Kolkata. Also active is Morgan Stanley, which closed a $150 million investment into

Oberoi Construction—a builder of apartments and commercial properties. The world's largest pension fund, CalPERS, which manages the retirement funds for California government employees, has announced that it is investing $400 million in Indian real estate.

If the Indian government allows free and open investment in most forms of real estate, this could become a much larger opportunity for Western firms.

Training and Education

Of foreign students in the United States, the largest number are from India. This tells you something both about the attractiveness of American university brands and about Indian spending power.

At present, foreign universities are allowed very limited access into India. But as we will see in chapter 4, "Human Resources," limitations on the availability of education continue to hold back hundreds of millions of young Indians. As the ecosystem allows more foreign participation on the ground, Western educational and training organizations will have an excellent opportunity to accelerate their presence in India. Rising aspirations in corporate India and among middle-class consumers could fuel explosive growth as tens of millions of citizens start to benefit from Western training and educational practices.

This can benefit foreign universities, once they are allowed to set up campuses in-country. It can also benefit companies and associations that provide training, learning, and job-related skills.

Conclusion

There is plenty of "white space" for Western companies to expand their revenues in India. There is also considerable opportunity to improve the productivity of funds deployed by leveraging Indian resources. Your head of sales and your CFO will love the Indian opportunity. Your marketing and human resource team will definitely have to stretch. And you may need to hire many biculturally savvy project managers, depending on your business.

But the real treasures will go to the CEOs who can transform their companies—and to the managers who show the way. Fortunately, the course is not as risky or murky as it was ten years ago when some bold American companies embarked upon this journey.

And it's worth noting a caution from John Triplett, the American executive based in Delhi for seven years: "More than one person in charge of a foreign company in India here has mentioned to me that the corporate office back home—be it the US, Europe, or Asia—does not understand why it takes so long to accomplish things here, why things go wrong, why regulations can change quickly here. Corporate should accept that the slow process of the system also works in their favor in that people here expect things to take time to resolve. The person in charge on the ground here in India needs support, not criticism. They need to internalize that patience is a necessity here, and that India is a commitment, not a fancy."

CHAPTER 2

India in Context

Before you can engage successfully with twenty-first-century India, it is crucial to get some perspective on what makes the country tick. That's the purpose of this chapter. We will rapidly review history, religion, and geography, but through the lens of an impatient American executive who wants a crash course.

Western executives unfamiliar with India's history sometimes ask me why there appears to be an undercurrent of disdain and concern toward the power of foreign companies in India. The answer is simple: India's early experience with a foreign company had its unpleasant side. The memory of that pain casts a shadow even today.

For one hundred years, much of India was ruled by the English East India Company, also called John Company. By many counts, it exercised more power at its peak than any modern-day corporation—more than Carnegie Steel, the Standard Oil Company, and the so-called robber barons of nineteenth-century America. While the East India Company was created by Queen Elizabeth I in the year 1600, for many decades it was one of several trading outfits from Europe vying for business and power along with dozens of powerful Indian merchants, mostly sole proprietors. The lines between politics and business were blurry, and many of the traders also maintained their own security or militia, even their own armies. Then one unlikely Englishman, Robert Clive, changed the landscape of eighteenth-century India.

In 1743, India was divided politically among many rulers. Eighteen-year-old Clive arrived in what is now Chennai as the lowliest employee of the John Company; by 1757, he was in the service of the British army as that force, with just three thousand men, defeated the ruler of Bengal and his army of fifty thousand in the battle of Plassey (Palashi to the local Bengalis). This victory established British military superiority over India. Clive became a hero and one of the wealthiest Britons of his time, allowing him to buy a seat in the British Parliament and an Irish peerage.

Under a royal monopoly for Indian trade, John Company collected taxes, ran the army, administered laws, and rapidly became the dominant power in India. Protected by British power, the company grew opium in India and exported it to China, even though Chinese law prohibited import of the addictive drug.

In the meantime, another Englishman, Charles Cornwallis, was fighting on the British side in the American Revolution. In 1781, at age forty-three, Cornwallis finally surrendered to American and French troops in the siege of Yorktown, Virginia, virtually ending the Revolutionary War.

But Corwallis returned to England, with his best days ahead of him in another colony. Just five years later, the East India Company had a top-level vacancy and hired Cornwallis, who had never been to India, as not only governor general of Bengal but also commander in chief of its army.

The Cornwallis Code formed the basis of revenue collection, justice administration, police systems, and more; its spirit survives in today's India. During this time, the John Company continued to ship Chinese silk and tea, along with Indian calico and indigo, while taxing Indian citizens on the collection, sale, and import of salt. According to UCLA historian Stanley Wolpert, "It was Cornwallis who was to be the true architect of John Company Raj [rule]."

The rule of the East India Company also brought to India some of the great dividends of the Industrial Revolution that was sweeping England: steam-powered trains, the electric telegraph, and a uniform national postal system. All along, the eastern port city of Kolkata (or Calcutta, as the British called it) in the province of Bengal was the capital of the British Raj. Industry, trade, culture, and the economy of India were generally weighted toward Bengal during these years. Over time, native Bengalis such as Dwarkanath Tagore—the senior partner of Carr, Tagore & Co., India's first biracial enterprise—also became major exporters, coal miners, and tea growers.

While the company enriched Clive, Cornwallis, their successors, their stockholders, and the British treasury, its harsh methods, insensitive practices, and inept policies impoverished and enraged most Indians. It often seemed incapable or uninterested in dealing with famines, strife, or disciplining corrupt officials.

A full century after Clive's victory at Plassey, there was a widespread rebellion against the rulers, in what the British described as the Sepoy Mutiny of 1857 and modern Indian history calls the First War for Independence. This led to the imposition of direct Crown rule by the British Parliament in 1858 and the eventual dissolution of the East India Company in 1874.

In some ways, the Indian psyche still equates foreign companies with subjugation and injustice. I advise my clients to make sure that their brand message and activities do not come afoul of this undercurrent no matter what product or service they want to sell in India today.

The Jewel in the Crown

Many of the laws and practices that govern India today were first promulgated by the Crown and retained after India became independent. Western attorneys and accountants, therefore, find some familiarity in modern India's practices. The elite Indian Civil Service was created as the instrument of the Crown, to collect taxes and keep the natives in check. It survives today as the Indian Administrative Service (IAS). Laws and taxes encouraged the export of India's resources and the import of English products, especially textiles, to the detriment of Indian businesses.

Under Crown rule, British companies were allowed to set up shop in India, and many did.

While American companies salivate at India's consumer market, I remind them that they are likely to start as the underdogs. That's because European companies had a head start.

For example, Unilever traces its roots in-country to 1888, when its predecessor began selling soap in India. Today, with thirty-six thousand employees, Hindustan Unilever (as it is now known) is India's largest consumer packaged goods company. It produces, distributes, and sells Kwality ice cream, Lifebuoy soap, Lipton tea, Pepsodent toothpaste, and Surf laundry detergent in addition to many products designed exclusively for India. The Imperial Tobacco Company began selling cigarettes in 1910 but diversified and Indianized over the years and is now called ITC Ltd.; it has expanded into hotels, information technology, packaging, foods, and more. With twenty thousand employees, it is also among India's top public companies.

Several of India's home-grown powerhouses also began life during colonial rule. Jamsetji Tata entered the textile business, and the Tata companies expanded into steel, chemicals, and aviation prior to India's independence. Ghanshyam Das Birla started in textiles as well, and his companies expanded into automobiles. Birla was a close confidant of Mohandas Karamchand Gandhi, India's most renowned freedom fighter, known as Mahatma Gandhi or simply *Bapu* (father).

According to economic historian Angus Maddison, in 1700 India controlled 24.4 percent of the world's GDP, more than all Western Europe. But by the time India became independent of British rule in 1947, Maddison estimates that India's share had diminished to just 4.2 percent. India's culture was not crushed, but its economic might had been marginalized, even vanquished forever, some might have concluded.

Independent India

Liberated India became a parliamentary democracy with a free press and guaranteed individual rights at midnight on August 15, 1947. The odd hour of the ceremony, incidentally, was a compromise between Viceroy Mountbatten's chosen date and Hindu astrologers, who deemed that anytime after about 2:00 AM would be terribly inauspicious.

India was free, but true economic revival and global business opportunity would take another forty-four years.

India's first prime minister, Jawaharlal Nehru, was a Fabian Socialist. During his seventeen-year tenure, the nation invested heavily into building companies owned by the government, and the term *public-sector company* entered the Indian vernacular. With a few notable exceptions, industrial planning and licensing replaced the Crown as the chokehold on Indian entrepreneurship. Insurance, railways, and airlines were nationalized; eventually, virtually any large company that began to falter would be taken over by the state. Incumbent foreign and domestic companies complained mildly about regulation but also became slothful and inefficient due to decades of limited competition.

The fourteen largest banks were nationalized in 1969 by Nehru's daughter Indira Gandhi, who was prime minister at the time. And in 1977, when the government forced multinationals to reduce their equity to less than 50 percent, both IBM and Coca-Cola decided to exit India. The British Raj had been replaced by the License Raj, and international business had almost written India off. Until 1991, the expansion of the government into the corporate sector continued, and India's annual economic growth seldom exceeded 4 percent.

The Elephant Reawakens

In July 1991, India's foreign exchange reserves were down to just two weeks' worth of imports. Black-market trading of gold, foreign currency, and smuggled imported consumer durables was rampant. Inflation was at 14 percent, overseas debt was rising, and creditors were getting restless. The ultimate humiliation came when the Indian government was forced to ship out a portion of its gold reserves to London as collateral against its debt. This crisis led to the fastest and most radical economic reforms in India's history.

Oxford and Cambridge economist Dr. Manmohan Singh had just been appointed finance minister at the time. Along with Commerce Minister P. Chidambaram, a Harvard MBA, and Commerce Secretary Montek Singh Ahluwalia, a Rhodes Scholar, he wrote and executed the dramatic changes. The rupee was devalued by 20 percent. Import tariffs—which often exceeded 100 percent of the value of the item being imported—were slashed to an average of 25 percent. Foreign institutional investors were allowed to invest in India's equity markets, and Indian firms were permitted to raise capital overseas. Overseas investors were permitted to take 100 percent equity stakes in some industries and 51 percent in many others. Limited privatization of some public-sector undertakings was implemented.

The results were dramatic. Economic growth rose to better than 6 percent, foreign investment increased, and companies from all over the first world made a beeline for India. India became a founding member of the World Trade Organization in 1995, six years ahead of China's entry.

Even though governments have changed five times since 1991, liberalization continues to move forward, if somewhat unsteadily. Remember, India is an elephant, not a tiger.

India Today

In 2007, India's GDP crossed the trillion-dollar line at official exchange rates. Based on purchasing power parity, India is just behind the United States, China, and Japan in GDP. In recent quarters, the Indian growth rate has edged above 9 percent. More than one hundred million Indians have been lifted out of poverty in the last decade.

In 2006, India exported $112 billion of goods and services while importing about $188 billion. Exports include gems and jewelry, engineering goods, chemicals, leather items, textile goods, and services. Besides oil and natural gas from the Middle East, India imports machinery, fertilizer, and chemicals in vast quantities. The United States, China, the United Kingdom, and Germany are major trading partners.

But per-capita income is still just $3,800, and more than three hundred million Indians survive on less than $1 per day. Hunger is a real problem, and millions of children die each year from diseases that are readily preventable. The specter of terrorism continues to haunt India, as it does the United States and the United Kingdom. And petty corruption saps the productivity of the Indian entrepreneur and manager. In fact, economic progress has by many accounts made some corrupt officials greedier.

Foreign aid, which sustained independent India in its first four decades, is now limited to very specific and narrow areas. In fact, immediately after the devastating Indian Ocean tsunami in 2004, India's military provided relief to neighboring countries. And on September 17, 2005, an Indian air force Ilyushin 76 landed at Little Rock Air Force Base in Arkansas bearing twenty-five tons of relief supplies for American victims of Hurricane Katrina. You may have missed the news, but it was on the front pages of the Indian media.

The elephant is feeling pretty confident. Some even detect a swagger in its step.

Polycultural Society

Most Indians associate the Golden Arches of McDonald's with the Maharaja Mac, a mutton burger, or the Aloo-Tikki Burger, a lovely blend of a local snack and an American concept. McDonald's is quite successful with upper-middle-class Indians today, but you won't find any Big Macs at its stores. In fact, vegetarian and nonvegetarian dishes are handled separately in its kitchens, with utensils and cooking oils never intermingled. This is because a large number of Indian Hindus are vegetarian, and eating beef is frowned upon by most Hindus.

Every time there is a religious riot in India, it makes global headlines. But this picture can be vastly misleading. In fact, every day hundreds of millions in India wear their religion on their sleeves and live peacefully together, while in the United States we often deal with diversity by down-playing cultural or other differences in the workplace. An Indian worker may have a screensaver of Lord Ganesha on his computer, or a statue of the Blessed Virgin Mary on her desk, or may step out to face Mecca and say Namaz several times a day. Indians celebrate diversity in the workplace and in the neighborhood. A colleague's religious festival is just one more reason to rejoice and share the joy.

A thousand years before the United States became the symbol of polyculturalism, India was already a happy blend of diverse religions. Let's take a look at people from some of the major religions in India and how their thinking may affect your business interests.

Hindus

More than eight hundred million Hindus live in India, which officially and practically is a secular country. Neighboring Nepal to the north is officially a Hindu state, and the Indonesian island of Bali is mostly Hindu. But most Western business people have not encountered this religion, and for most it is imperative that they understand it.

It often confounds those curious about Hinduism that there isn't one definitive high priest, holy book, conversion process, or official version of Hinduism. Surprisingly to most who are new to India, it's not against the Hindu religion to pray in a Christian church or to revere Moses or Christ. My cousin-in-law is a devoted Hindu and visits St. Anthony's Church in Worli, Mumbai, regularly. She says, "They have a statue of Anthony holding the baby Jesus. It is thought that the saint conveys to Jesus the problems of poor and sick people." Many residents of Mumbai also believe that if you lose something valuable, you may get it back if you pray at this little church.

My own Hindu parents saw no conflict in sending me for eleven years to a school run by the Methodist Church in Kanpur, and my wife, Smita, was mostly educated by Catholic nuns. She and I are more familiar with the Ten Commandments and the Sermon on the Mount than our California-raised children are.

Hindus believe in one all-pervasive, supreme God who may be worshipped in many different forms and by different names, as either male or female. The religion is better described as henotheistic, rather than polytheistic. Henotheism recognizes that other gods may exist and can be worshipped; this tenet probably underlies the success of tolerance and diversity in India.

The proper name of the Hindu religion is *Santana Dharma,* which roughly translates into "the eternal or universal values in life that sustain us all." Its ultimate scriptures are four ancient Vedas, which were passed down verbally for centuries before being transcribed. But most Hindus do not read or study the Vedas. Tales of the incarnations of Lord Vishnu, such as Ram and Krishna, are plentiful in modern Indian folklore. Two great epics, Valmiki's *Ramayana* and Vyas's *Mahabharata,* embody many Hindu teachings in the form of stories and are each at least twenty-five hundred years old. Indian children, regardless of their religion, grow up with these stories as part of the culture. In fact, when Bollywood directors converted these epics into seventy-eight- and ninety-four-episode series, respectively, they became the most-watched TV shows of all time in India.

The *Srimad Bhagvad Gita* or *Gita* is often called the essence of Hinduism and is contained with the *Mahabharata.* The epic has influenced many Americans, including the inventor of the atomic bomb, J. Robert Oppenheimer, who invoked it when he witnessed the fury of the first mushroom cloud in the New Mexico desert.

To introduce Hinduism, I often start the executive seminar that I teach on business in India with an image of 21,778-foot-tall Mount Kailash, located in Tibet. This ice-topped rock is the mythical home of Lord Shiva, the most powerful deity in the Hindu pantheon. Shiva is also known as Mahesh (chief god), and he is reputed to have 1,008 other names. While he has the power to destroy the entire universe with his dance of death, Lord Shiva is also a simpleton known as Bholanath (the innocent one). His gullibility is celebrated in Hindu myths. Shiva is worshipped in phallic form throughout India.

Oxford University Professor Gavin Flood describes Shiva as a god of ambiguity and paradox. As a Western executive, if you can begin to appreciate ambiguity and paradox, you can start to grapple with India.

Female deities play a central role in Hinduism, including Shiva's consort Parvati, also known as Durga. In her form as Kali, she was worshipped before battles. There is Lakshmi, the goddess of wealth and plenty, the consort of Lord Vishnu, and a favorite of business people. There is Saraswati, the goddess of wisdom and learning, who is the consort of Lord Brahma.

One of Shiva and Parvati's two sons is Lord Ganesha, who has the head of an elephant and a corpulent human body. You will see his pictures and statues everywhere in modern India.

Each god in Hinduism has an animal that he or she rides; Ganesha is assigned the mouse. A story is told about a race around the world among the minor gods. The winner would be the first god invoked in all future prayers. The clever Ganesha knew that his mouse could not keep up with the peacocks, tigers, and horses—but like many modern Indians, he had a witty workaround or *jugaad*.

He simply rode around his parents three times and told them, "For me, you, my dear parents, are my entire world." He was declared the winner. Even today, all Hindu services begin with an invocation to the god who used his elephant mind. Many Indian entrepreneurs and executives, regardless of their religion, pride themselves on and attribute their success to such bold thinking and cleverness.

Hindus believe that the soul is immortal and it experiences varied lives through which it evolves spiritually. In the Hindu way of thinking, karma is the universal law of cause and effect; each action has a reaction. The cycle is endless, with souls carrying their karma into future lives. The *Gita* teaches Hindus to remain unattached to the fruits of their virtuous actions.

There are many symbols for the Hindu religion, such as the sacred word *Om* (Aum) and images of the various gods, but one in particular that can be confusing to Western business people is the ancient symbol of the *satiya*, more commonly known as the swastika. The Nazis adopted it as their symbol in 1920 as the *Hakenkreuz*, or hooked cross. I particularly caution my Jewish clients that they will see the *satiya* all over India in Hindu, Jain, and even in some Buddhist sites. It has no connection to the events of the German Third Reich.

Western executives new to India often ask about the Hindu caste system. There are four major castes, based on ancient occupations: Brahmins who used to be priests, Kshatriyas who used to be warriors and law enforcers, Vaishyas who used to be business people, and Shudras who were laborers. Each caste has thousands of subgroups. Marriage between castes was historically frowned upon but is becoming more common in urban India. Today, members of any caste can pursue any profession. Members of certain "scheduled" castes that were historically disadvantaged are allocated special quotas and preferences in government jobs, college admissions, and seats in legislatures. In hiring, promotion, marketing, and vendor practices in India, most Western companies can ignore a person's caste almost completely. The reality is that most foreign business people don't need to worry much about caste in modern-day India.

Hinduism has survived the rise of other religions in India, including Buddhism, Jainism, Islam, and Christianity. It has evolved and continues to evolve in twenty-first-century India.

Muslims

If you are a customer of Wipro, one of India's top three information technology companies, you have already been influenced by billionaire Azim Premji, who owns 80 percent of the company. If you buy generic medications in the United States, you are probably a customer of Dr. Yusuf K. Hamied's company, Cipla. The $800 million pharmaceutical company exports more than half its products. While you cannot buy her products readily in the United States, the owner of India's largest herbal products company is Shahnaz Husain. Premji, Hamied, and Husain are Muslims, or followers of Islam.

When you turn on the television in India or look at the billboards along the streets, you will likely see the face of leading Bollywood star Shah Rukh Khan, who has endorsed dozens of products, from cars to computers, cell phone services, electronics, and luxury watches. Bollywood, as India's $6 billion entertainment industry is often called, is full of successful Muslim directors, writers, and performers.

India is home to more Muslims than Saudi Arabia, Iraq, Iran, and Syria put together. In fact, only Indonesia and Pakistan have more followers of the Islamic faith than India. It is India's second largest religion. You will see mosques in every major city, and you may hear the call to prayer as you pass them. While Western media often portrays "Hindu India" pitted against Muslim Pakistan, the reality on the ground is quite different. Muslims are well integrated into the fabric of Indian business, national, political, and social life. Three Muslims have been elected president; tens of thousands serve in the armed forces. Muslim directors have created some of Bollywood's most patriotic films, such as the 2004 feature *Lakshya,* set against the backdrop of the Kargil conflict in Kashmir.

Islam first came to the west coast of India via Arab traders shortly after the time of the prophet Muhammad. Invaders from the Middle East brought Islam to north India and, by the twelfth century, had established control of Delhi with the sultanate.

Historically, Islam has had a tremendous influence in India, the pinnacle of which was the Moghul empire. This dynasty dominated northern India from 1526 to 1761 and left behind some of India's most recognizable monuments and modern tourist attractions, including the Taj Mahal in Agra and the Red Fort in Delhi. In the south, Hyderabad is home to the four-spired mosque Charminar, built in 1591 and considered the symbol of this large city.

Indian Muslims include Sunnis and Shias, much as in the rest of the world. Members of a sect within the Shia, known as the Ismailis, are followers of the Aga Khan. Many Ismailis from Gujarat and Rajasthan belong to the Khoja clan, and many may retain Hindu names. There is also a strong Sufi, or mystic, tradition in India. In fact, the tomb of twelfth-century Sufi saint Khawaja Moinuddin Chishti in the city of Ajmer is revered by Muslims and Hindus alike and is one of most popular sites in the northern state of Rajasthan.

While India is diverse and tolerant, religious sensitivities run high, and business people need to be careful of offending any religion. Sir Salman Rushdie, Booker Prize–winning author of *Midnight's Children,* published *The Satanic Verses* on September 26, 1988, which many Muslims found offensive. Just nine days later, India became the first country to ban the book. This happened a full four months before global controversy erupted when Ayatollah Khomeini of Iran issued an order to assassinate Rushdie.

Christians

Today there are twenty-five million Christians in India, making it India's third largest religion, but India welcomed the religion well before Europe did.

It is believed that the Apostle Judas Thomas ("Doubting Thomas" from the Last Supper) migrated to India in the year 52 CE and traveled the country seeking converts. He is buried at the Basilica of St. Thomas in Chennai. Descendants from this thread of Christianity are generally known as Syrian Christians in India and are sometimes called Nasranis.

Portuguese explorer Vasco da Gama found the sea route to India by sailing around the Cape of Good Hope in 1498. European missionaries soon followed and established a base for Christianity in western India, with a large concentration in Goa; most of these converts are Roman Catholics. Goa remained a Portuguese territory until 1961, fourteen years after India became independent.

Protestant missionaries from the United Kingdom arrived in significant numbers in the nineteenth century after the East India Company had been dismantled. They set up hospitals and orphanages in addition to churches. Indians of all religions often prefer to send their children to private "convent schools," the term used loosely to refer to schools run by any Christian church. Many of the business leaders with whom you may interact in India are the products of such Christian schools.

Christian business people include Vinoo Mammen, the CEO of MRF Ltd., India's largest tire maker. The current defense minister, A. K. Antony of Kerala, is probably the most prominent Christian in India today. Gracias Saldanha, founder of Glenmark Pharmaceuticals, is a billionaire and a Christian; as is Hollywood producer and former Wimbledon tennis star Ashok Amritraj, who has created hits such as *Bringing Down the House.*

Sikhs

Sikhs number more than twenty-three million, but over 90 percent of them live in the northern state of Punjab, where they are close to 65 percent of the population. By Indian standards, Sikhism is a young religion; its founder, Guru Nanak, lived from 1469 to 1530. The tenth and final Sikh guru (teacher) encoded the beliefs of the religion into a scripture called the Guru Granth Sahib. Most Sikh men have the last name or middle name *Singh* (which means "lion"), and most Sikh girls use the middle or last name *Kaur* until they are married.

Incidentally, adventurous Sikh farmers were among the first Indian immigrants to North America, starting more than a hundred years ago. One of them, Dalip Singh Saund, rose to fame when he became the first Indian American to win a seat in the House of Representatives in 1955, just nine years after the United States passed a law permitting Indians to apply for citizenship.

Billionaires Malvinder and Shivinder Singh are the largest stockholders in pharmaceutical company Ranbaxy Labs, based in Gurgaon, near New Delhi. The former chief of India's army, General Joginder "JJ" Singh, and the current prime minister of India, Dr. Manmohan Singh, are Sikhs as well.

If you are in business in India, you had better not even consider banning facial hair or headgear—Sikhs are required to leave their hair uncut, and most wear turbans. Sikhs living in the West have fought and won many court actions to assert their freedom to express their religious beliefs without workplace discrimination.

Jains

If you've bought a diamond in recent years, it's very likely that regardless of its origin in South Africa, the rock was cut and polished by one of the three hundred thousand workers in Surat, India, where a small community, the Palanpuri Jains, have set up operations that rival Antwerp and Tel Aviv. Diamond merchant Vijay Shah of VijayDimon is a press-shy Jain whose holdings span Europe, Asia, and North America.

Billionaire widow Indu Jain owns a substantial portion of the stock of Bennett Coleman & Company, which publishes the *Times of India*. Pradeep Jain holds 80 percent of northern India's Parsvnath Developers, which owns more than 120 million square feet of real estate. After his company went public, he also became a billionaire.

It is important that you understand the twelve-million-strong Jain religion in India because of its significance in business. The western states of Maharashtra, Rajasthan, and Gujarat have the largest Jain population. About twenty-six hundred years old, this religion promotes nonviolence and stringent vegetarianism. Jains refuse food obtained with unnecessary cruelty. Some are vegan due to the perceived violence of modern dairy farms, and others exclude root vegetables, such as potatoes, onions, and garlic, from their diets in order to preserve the lives of the plants from which they eat. Some Jain business people who travel overseas pack several days of meals with them since they can't be sure of finding food that is appropriate for them.

Jains and Hindus intermarry freely, and Jains celebrate many Hindu festivals. Some Hindus may tell you that Jainism is a sect within Hinduism, but that is inaccurate.

Zoroastrians

Zoroastrianism was once the dominant religion of much of what is now Iran; it is perhaps three thousand years old. With the rise of Islam in Persia, some Zoroastrians fled to the shores of Gujarat in western India. According to one legend, when they asked for permission to stay from the local ruler, he sent them back a full cup of milk to signify that there was no room for new immigrants. The leader of the group returned the milk with some sugar added, and the message, "We will sweeten your community and not take up any additional space." And so it has been for hundreds of years. Parsis, as these arrivals came to be called, have thrived in India and have created jobs, given back in charity, and set new benchmarks in global business. There are fewer than a quarter million Zoroastrians worldwide, but they have a significant presence in India and their influence is felt by hundreds of millions of Indians daily.

The Tata group of companies is one of India's largest and most respected business conglomerates, with twenty-eight publicly listed entities and ninety-six operating companies. Its chairman is Ratan Tata, a Parsi. If you deal with India, it won't be long before you see a Tata car or truck. With $22 billion in sales, the group is a leader in fields as diverse as software services, automobiles, steel, energy, and hospitality.

Two years before steel magnate Andrew Carnegie gave a million dollars to set up what is now Carnegie Mellon University, the enterprising founder of the Tata group had pledged *half* of his wealth to create what eventually became the Indian Institute of Science in Bangalore. The Tata trusts continue to fund charities of every ilk imaginable, from hospitals to cultural centers and sports groups, and they control 65 percent of the stock of the holding company Tata Sons. The Tata.com Web site asserts, "The trusteeship principle governing the way the group functions casts the Tatas in a rather unique light: capitalistic by definition but socialistic by character." *Socialistic by character*: Try finding such words on Donald Trump's or Warren Buffett's site. The Indian elephant is unique indeed!

Other prominent Zoroastrian business people include billionaire Adi Godrej, whose companies produce soaps, home appliances, hair dyes, and office furniture. Nusli Wadia is a textile magnate; the Wadia family also runs the Miss India pageant.

Buddhists

Most Westerners associate Buddhism with China and Japan, but the religion originated in northern India in the fifth century BCE. While it was once dominant in the nation, it is now far more common outside its birthplace. Many Hindus regard its founder, Gautama Buddha, as one of their deities. Buddhism continues to be practiced in the northeastern states of India. In 1956, when Mao Zedong sent the People's Liberation Army into Tibet, Buddhist leader the Dalai Lama sought and received refuge in India, where he still lives.

Jews

The first Jews came to India at least twenty-five hundred years ago; there have since been five separate migrations of different Jewish populations to India. While the numbers are small, you will find Jewish populations and synagogues in Mumbai, Cochin, and the eastern state of Mizoram.

Jewish business people flourished with the rise of Mumbai under the British Crown. Sir Victor Sassoon was one of the most successful businessmen in Mumbai, and his family company, E. D. Sassoon & Co., had a thriving trade. However, worried about the Indian independence movement, he moved his headquarters to Shanghai, where he built the world-famous Cathay Hotel on the Bund. Sassoon lived to see the Japanese occupation of Shanghai, followed by the takeover of his fortune and his hotel by the People's Liberation Army in 1949. History may have taken Sassoon down a different path had he stayed in India.

Bahá'í Religion

There are only about five million Bahá'ís worldwide, and a very small number in India. Still, one of the most spectacular modern buildings in New Delhi is the Bahá'í House of Worship, more commonly known as the Lotus Temple. Since the temple's opening in 1987, it has become a major attraction for people of all religions. It is often compared to the Taj Mahal in its majesty and splendor.

The Lay of the Land

I have definitely learned that India is a big country and a cultural divide exists from place to place. Bangalore is very different to Delhi.

—David Bradley, head of Indian sales for a
$10 billion US company

The Indian subcontinent is located in South Asia and separated from the rest of Asia by the tallest mountain range in the world, the Himalayas, formed when the Deccan landmass rammed into the rest of Asia about fifty-five million years ago.

Shaped roughly like a baseball diamond, the northwest is bordered by Pakistan—with which it has fought multiple wars, mostly over disputed parts of Kashmir. Most of the northeastern edge of the diamond is bordered by Nepal and China. China briefly invaded India in October 1962.

The southwestern edge of the baseball diamond is the Arabian Sea. Here the port city of Mumbai, formerly known as Bombay, is the financial, industrial, and entertainment nerve center of India, and the largest city by population. If you are going to engage India in any major way, you would do well to spend time in this city.

MAXIMUM CITY

Novelist Suketu Mehta won the Kiriyama Prize for his 1999 title *Maximum City*, which describes the joys and horrors of modern-day Mumbai. Forty years earlier my father, an urban geographer, wrote his doctoral thesis on this marvelous megalopolis.

In many ways, Mumbai represents the business essence of India. More than a third of all personal income taxes collected in India come from this one city. The corporate tax ratio is even higher, but that is partly because so many large national companies are headquartered here, including Grasim Industries, ICICI Bank, Larsen & Toubro, Mahindra & Mahindra, State Bank of India, Tata Consultancy Services, Tata Steel, Tata Motors, and Videocon.

The most prolific movie industry in the world, now known as Bollywood, is centered in Mumbai. While yet to make a major impact in the West, these musical extravaganzas actually draw more eyeballs across Asia and Africa each year than Hollywood does.

One of the largest slums in the world, Dharavi, is located in Mumbai, as is some of India's most expensive real estate, at Nariman Point. Extreme opulence and shocking poverty collide across the crushing city of seven interconnected islands and choking traffic. Almost twenty million people live in and around Mumbai. But infrastructure improvement projects of breathtaking scope are in progress as I write this, including the Bandra Worli Sea Link Project, an eight-lane road and bridge over Mahim Bay that will shave at least thirty minutes off the excruciating drive from downtown Mumbai to the airport.

While the local population of Mumbai is Maharashtrian (people from the Indian state of Maharashtra), the city has attracted large numbers from other states, including Gujaratis (from Gujarat), Biharis (from Bihar), Tamils, Punjabis, UP-wallahs (from Uttar Pradesh), and more. It is truly cosmopolitan.

Mumbai has the pace of Manhattan and, like Manhattan, it has swiftly sprung back in the face of immense tragedy. When an incredible thirty-seven inches of rain deluged the city on July 26, 2005, Mumbaikars (as local residents are called) shook themselves dry in a few days and went right back to work. When terrorists in suburban trains set off seven separate explosions during the course of just eleven minutes on July 11, 2006, killing more than two hundred people, the local residents immediately rallied together to help.

Mumbai is an overwhelming, exciting, confusing, and energetic place, one that often evokes extreme reactions from first-time visitors. If your reaction is to recoil and back off, I urge you to persist and engage; you may change your mind.

The southeastern edge of the baseball diamond borders the Bay of Bengal. At first base is India's second largest city, now known as Kolkata, formerly Calcutta. It was the capital under the British Raj until 1911. Marwari entrepreneurs, including the Birlas and the Goenkas from the western part of the country, came here to thrive in the jute, cotton, and tea trades, but stayed on to build car factories, media empires, and more. The state of West Bengal where Kolkata is located has been run by one of the Communist Parties since the late 1970s. Western companies have only recently begun to invest there.

India's capital of New Delhi and its twin city, Delhi, are near the pitcher's mound on our baseball diamond. Much of the industrial growth around the capital territory is actually located in the neighboring states of Haryana (Gurgaon and Faridabad) and Uttar Pradesh (Noida). Large business groups headquartered around Delhi include Bharti Airtel, Hero Honda, and HCL, as well as the largest carmaker in India, Maruti Suzuki.

On the southern coast, facing the Bay of Bengal, is Chennai, known for automotive companies such as truck and bus maker Ashok Leyland, tire producer MRF, and ancillary suppliers the TVS Group. Hyundai, Ford, BMW, and Mitsubishi also have plants in the area.

Two hundred miles inland from Chennai and at a much cooler altitude is Bangalore, often called the Silicon Valley of India thanks to companies like Infosys, Wipro, and IBM. Bangalore is also home to the headquarters of Hindustan Aeronautics Ltd. (H.A.L.) and Bharat Electronics Ltd. (B.E.L.); both are large public-sector companies. Bangalore's year-round pleasant weather has also attracted dozens of European and American companies such as GE, Intel, Philips, and Siemens. North of Bangalore is another major city, Hyderabad, home to Dr. Reddy's Laboratories—a top pharmaceutical company—and IT outsourcer Satyam Computer Services.

Overseas companies may also find it worthwhile to consider second-tier cities such as Pune, well connected to Mumbai by India's first limited-access highway. Other second-tier cities include Trivandrum (also called Thiruvananthapuram), on the Kerala coast; Nagpur, in the geographic center of the country, where Boeing is investing $100 million in a repair facility; Chandigarh, a planned city in Punjab; Ahmedabad, home to some of the most entrepreneurial Indians; and Indore in Madhya Pradesh.

Government

In July 2007, Jeffrey Immelt, the CEO of General Electric, one of the most successful American companies in India, said, "The economy in India is now at the point where the government can't screw it up any longer."

Michael Ducker, president international of FedEx, would agree, "Since 2005, I have noticed that the administration has become more focused, more disciplined. They are also open to talking about business interests and are very interested in India's economic development and in building the country up." Ducker, incidentally, has the unique perspective of being a board member of both the US–India Business Council and the US–China Business Council.

India is a parliamentary democracy with a federal system that is formally a union of twenty-six states. The legislative, executive, and judicial branches of government function in a balance of power that is similar to Western democracies. The civil services led by the elite Indian Administrative Service have considerable power over the functioning of the government. Secretaries in most federal and state ministries are typically IAS officers. For major business deals that involve the government, you will need to understand the civil services as well as, if not better than, the leadership.

The prime minister heads the Union Government, often called the Central Government. Like the British PM, he or she can be replaced anytime by Parliament. There are, incredibly, more than fifty ministries, from obviously important ones such as Defense and External Affairs to the nearly obscure, like the Ministry of Earth Sciences or the Ministry of Statistics. Ministers in India are the rough equivalent of cabinet secretaries in the United States, but all ministers must be members of one of the houses of Parliament. The president in India is largely a ceremonial figure—but in the case of a hung Parliament, he or she does have the power to invite a specific person to form a government.

Powers that don't rest with the Central Government are handled by the state governments led by elected chief ministers, who are roughly akin to governors of American states. Depending on the nature of your business, some states may be more hospitable than others. Policies regarding employment, land incentives, and attitudes toward foreign investment vary from state to state. Also, some states are more politically stable than others. In some, a change in government does not imply major new policy directions that you may care about. In other states, though, such a change could put your project in jeopardy.

There are hundreds of political parties in India. At the national level, the Indian National Congress, the Bharatiya Janata Party, and the Communist Party of India (Marxist) are currently the strongest. But numerous regional parties are quite powerful in a particular state or region: the Akali Dal in Punjab, the Samajwadi Party and Bahujan Samaj Party in Uttar Pradesh, Dravida Munnetra Kazhagam (DMK) in Tamil Nadu, the Shiv Sena in Maharashtra . . . the list goes on. I tell my American clients to think of parties in India as we might think of spin-off companies in the United States.

In recent years, weak coalition governments have become the order of the day in India. An attitude of *Throw out the incumbents* has, at many elections, replaced the pre-1991 tendency to support the party in power.

In dealing with the government in India, foreign companies need to remember that they must deal primarily with the bureaucracy, at the federal (central), state, and local levels.

The political leadership provides the vision and sets policy but generally will not get involved in routine procedural decisions. Coalition politics implies considerable compromise; it can take a while for policies to form, and still longer for them to become reality.

WORKING ON WEEKENDS!

On one of our expansion initiatives, we were required to obtain a series of sequential (not parallel) approvals, and our time frame was very tight. I remember going into the state-run Software Technology Parks of India (STPI) after staying up much of the night filling out the application. A very dynamic woman ran it in Chennai. She was sitting across the table from me. I had my certified check and all the application papers before me. I asked, "How fast can this be processed?"

She answered, "Well, I will try to get it back to you in about three weeks."

"Three weeks! We need to get it down faster, please . . ."

She said, "Well, if I tell the staff, I can probably get it done in two weeks."

We had premised our whole corporate structure on this approval; it and all the remaining approvals had to be obtained in the next thirty days to meet a government deadline. I confided, "If we don't get this, we are going to be nothing."

I think I must have started getting very emotional at this point. I remember picking up what I thought was a blank paper in front of me and ripping it to shreds: "We'll be nothing, nothing, nothing!" She looked at me, horrified, and I just looked down at my hands. It was my certified cashier's check!

The very next day—it was a Saturday—STPI called me and and told me to come down for my approval.

—Joe Sigelman, founder of OfficeTiger (now part of
    RR Donnelley)

Corruption and the Underground Economy

Unlike some third-world countries, India is not a banana republic for sale to the highest bidder. While there have been some charges of bribery at the highest levels in the past, today there is much more transparency thanks to a vibrant press, a weak Central Government that can't be sure of staying in power for decades, and new laws that require openness.

At the lower strata of society, you may encounter drivers, peons, and others who ask for small tips or *baksheesh*. While irritating to those who are not used to it, and technically illegal in some cases (railway workers who are simply doing their jobs, certain employees who are not supposed to ask for tips), this behavior is not a serious snag to most business people.

It's everything between the two extremes that can be a problem. Officials may not be eager to move your file until they are paid. Inspectors may show up at your location and start citing your company for reasonable or unreasonable issues. Procurement staff may let your competitors take a peek at your "sealed" bid to give them a chance to preempt you. You may be subject to repeated and unnecessary audits.

It is possible to run an honest and clean business in India today. But corruption is certainly a factor. According to entrepreneur Arjun Malhotra, "Most foreign companies don't get involved. If they have a local partner, they let the partner take care of this issue. There are marketing agents in India, and some of them also help promote your cause with the government."

India does not recognize formal lobbyists, but some of these agents provide that role. If you are selling in the defense sector, be advised that agents are highly restricted.

A few American companies have told me that US laws and practices, such as the Foreign Corrupt Practices Act, actually work in their favor in India. Since the players are already aware that an American company cannot make unauthorized payments, everyone knows not to ask.

A related factor in India is the underground or "black" economy. Money from bribes, as well as undeclared revenue to evade taxes are sources of this parallel undocumented economy. In a 2002 book titled *The Black Economy in India,* Arun Kumar estimated that in 1996, the underground economy was about 40 percent of the size of its documented counterpart.

A 2007 World Bank report concluded that complex and costly business regulations push workers into the underground economy. "In India, over 8 million workers have formal jobs in the private sector—in a country of over 1 billion people and a work force of 458 million. In Northern European countries, where it is easy to do business and people benefit from social protection, less than 8% of all economic activity occurs in the underground economy." The same report, however, found that in 2007, India was the top reformer in South Asia.

Since this money is undocumented, people cannot deposit it into regular bank accounts. Some of it gets invested overseas. Much of it goes into under-invoiced real estate deals. A large proportion makes it way into lavish consumption. Many such transactions in India involve payment in currency notes. Over time, Indians have developed elaborate means to convert black money into "white."

Conclusion

Globalization in India began many hundreds of years ago. In this chapter, I have given you a bird's-eye view of the nation's history. With a view toward business interests only, we have looked at religious diversity and geographic complexity. You now have some understanding of a few of India's major companies, and I hope you can already see that India offers a lot more than outsourcing and information technology to the world. We have also touched upon the evolving role of government and of politics in India, and we've seen how some aspects of twenty-first-century India still feel like the nineteenth. Any one of these subjects could fill an entire book, of course, but you should now have enough context to start understanding the elephant.

CHAPTER 3

Cross-Cultural Communication

As Western companies and executives approach today's India, they trip up most often on cross-cultural issues. Sometimes it's because of their recent history: Many American companies focused on Japan and China in the 1980s and 1990s and now attempt to apply the learning from those cross-cultural experiences to India. For the most part, this doesn't work.

India Inc.'s marketing machine would have you believe that you might have no trouble communicating when you do business in India—after all, they speak English over there, right? Actually, that's an unsafe assumption for most Westerners, on several counts. First, the use of English masks the underlying differences and accentuates the possibility of cross-cultural conflict. Second, English is spoken differently in India than it is in the West. And third, effective cross-cultural communication isn't so much about food, clothing, manners, music, and arts as it is about attitudes, gender roles, communication styles, and—in the case of India—yes, language. Joe Sigelman, former CEO of

OfficeTiger, quips, "HSBC ads in jetways around the world tell you how a certain gesture in one country is insulting in another. Rubbish! That stuff doesn't really matter when you are in India."

"Many foreigners, when they come to India, operate on bad assumptions. If you come to India assuming most people or organizations are corrupt or can't be trusted, you are already in trouble and won't be successful," reasons Mason Byles, who spent several years in India on a joint-venture project with Hewlett-Packard in the 1990s. According to Byles, American arrogance is another problem; if you assume that you have the solutions before understanding the problems, and if you like to tell people how things should be done rather than asking sincerely for input in a way that will result in honest advice, you are doomed to fail. Some foreigners in India have a tendency to complain about the differences rather than to adapt, appreciate, and enjoy them—and that, too, is a recipe for failure.

Guy Rabbat grew up in Europe, where he worked for IBM, and now divides his time between south India and California. He declares, "As an American, if you want to be successful in India, stop on the way in London if you can." Indians have picked up many habits and processes from the British during the two hundred years of British rule.

Interestingly, many Indians tell me that they have an easier time working with many non-English Europeans than they do with many Americans. The success of European companies such as SKF, ABB, Philips, Siemens, and Alstom appears to support this mode of thinking. However, my own experience is that North American executives who are alert to cross-cultural communication can share the kind of success that Rabbat, Byles, and Sigelman have enjoyed in their ongoing dealings with India.

India will give you plenty to complain about on a daily basis. The objective of this chapter is to equip you to cope more effectively with India and Indians. Every time you encounter a frustrating experience, my first bit of advice is to pause and take a deep breath. Then, withhold judgment. Ask yourself if it is possible that this behavior or situation, which you find so offensive, might be perfectly normal in Indian culture. Of course, this is much harder to do than it is to say, but it gets easier with practice.

In this chapter, we'll talk about the Indian view of time, about social hierarchy in the workplace, about direct and indirect communication, and about building relationships with Indians. We'll also look at the real impact of superstition and religion on business as well as the implications of communicating in *Indian* English. We'll briefly discuss appearance, manners, and Indian names. With this backdrop, we finally examine negotiating with Indians, which properly belongs in this chapter and not in the legal discussion later in the book.

Indian Time

Time travels in divers paces with divers persons. I'll tell you who Time ambles withal, who Time trots withal, who Time gallops withal, and who he stands still withal.

—Rosalind, Act III, Scene ii, *As You Like It,*
by William Shakespeare

Many of my management consulting engagements result from the different perceptions of time in the West
compared with India.

In the West, we are accustomed to the sanctity of appointment times. In New York, being five minutes late to
an appointment is a major faux pas. But you may find that
Indians have a much more relaxed attitude toward punc-
tuality. If you are fifteen minutes late for a business appointment, people scarcely notice. If you show up on time
for a social engagement, you might be the first to arrive;
even the host may appear at least half an hour late. "Just
because someone makes me wait thirty minutes to see
them does not mean I am not important to them" was one
of the first cross-cultural lessons learned by David Bradley
when he moved to Asia and took over Indian sales at his
company in summer 2007.

"Often, Indians aren't making a real commitment when
they establish a schedule or target date. Slippages or re-
schedules are frequent—apparently without awareness
of the degree to which this behavior affects confidence
and trust," notes Don Hollis, who made seven trips to India
over a thirteen-month period while he was an executive at
check printer Deluxe.

Mason Byles wisely advises, "Don't assume, if an individual or organization makes a commitment that something is going to be done, that it will actually happen until you have established a track record with the individual or organization." You need to ask how the plan is going to be accomplished, and you need to get evidence that those you're working with have the experience to complete it. Discuss what might go wrong, and make contingency plans in case things do get off track. Hold frequent checkpoint meetings that include hard evidence of progress—more frequent than you might be used to, at least until you have established a track record. It is important that all of this be done in a way that builds trust and does not attack an individual or organization's credibility. The effort should be framed in terms of building a relationship or partnership.

With the right degree of management and active listening skills, it is possible to get projects completed on time or even ahead of schedule. The most celebrated recent example of this is the Delhi Metro transit system, which was completed three years ahead of schedule by a quasi-government agency. While many projects do run late and over budget, there are now plenty of teams quite adept at timely delivery, given proper cross-cultural oversight.

On a trade mission to India, some senior government officials kept my business team waiting for forty-five minutes while the staff checked our passports and shuffled papers. Some of our team members started to get restless; others felt slighted and wanted to leave. I counseled them that the delay was normal; our hosts were not trying to give us a *Yankee, go home* signal. I later received independent feedback from inside sources that the Indian officials were actually quite eager for and appreciative of our visit. It turned out to be one of the most productive meetings of the trip.

Don't schedule yourself too tightly when you are in India. If you have a working BlackBerry or cell phone, you can keep yourself productively occupied while you wait. Adapt, don't protest. Most Indians adjust to surprises on a daily basis. The faster you learn to do the same, the more direct will be your route to success.

Experts describe India as a polychronic culture, where time is viewed as a flexible, cyclical commodity, in plentiful supply. Let me give you an example. I walked into a neighborhood Airtel phone store in Kanpur, the city where I was born. The service person had two different customers sitting in front of her, but she immediately interrupted her conversation with one of them to hear my problem. The other two waited calmly while she and I spoke. Then she turned back to them and started to help them. She was not reacting to my perceived higher social status, however. In fact, she was simply multitasking and functioning in her normal way. I watched as she took several thousand rupees in cash (the equivalent of several hundred dollars) from one of the customers while simultaneously talking with Airtel phone support for the other customer; at the same time she motioned for me to place my phone on her desk and tried to jiggle its battery so she could continue helping me.

In the West, we are socialized to wait our turn. We also

expect undivided attention once we do start to be served. These are foreign concepts in India today. This woman's ability to multitask may actually maximize customer throughput. Remember this next time someone elbows past you while you are patiently waiting in line, anywhere in India. Indeed, if you have traveled in-country, you might chuckle at the previous sentence, because lines are almost never respected by Indians.

Arjun Malhotra, CEO of Headstrong, travels back and forth between India and the United States. He theorizes as to why Indians may be better at taking care of unexpected events and multiple variables whereas on the American side, people tend to be univariate. "The Hindu religion, dominant in India, is all about gray, whereas Judeo-Christianity is more about black and white. But since 99 percent of life is gray, perhaps Indians can be more adaptable."

Hierarchy and Power Distance

A senior Indian executive at a major multinational in India who deals with American colleagues and counterparts on a daily basis shared the following with me: "A cultural difference arises from a deeply socially hierarchical thinking among most Indians. Seniority and age count more than merit, sometimes at a subconscious level. Also, respect for elders sometimes inhibits open discussions." He advised that Americans need to understand but not accept this. They should encourage respect but let merit on the issues dominate the discussions, as they would in the West.

When Mason Byles returned to India after retiring from Hewlett-Packard to help run a school in Tamil Nadu, he had a difficult time adjusting to how rapidly plans transformed, with things added, eliminated, and modified. "Plans frequently changed as a result of someone high in the organization proposing an idea for consideration and having it interpreted lower in the organization as a directive for action. Individuals in India are reluctant to question authority."

When you manage Indians, you will likely find that there is a strong tendency to only want to deliver good news, tell you what is going well, and ignore what is going badly. People may tell you what they think you want to hear, not what they really feel about an issue. To overcome such behavior, to encourage straight talk, and to receive a reliable flow of bad news, you will need to establish multiple channels of communication and allocate plenty of casual, social time.

John Triplett, former India managing director of consulting firm Parsons, worked in Delhi on a multicultural team of 160 engineers, including just 20 expatriates. Triplett inspired them all to work closely as a team and take joint responsibility for all decisions. "Ninety percent of the time we took the right decision. When we were wrong, we never, never looked for guilt. This surprised the Indians at first, but very soon the entire team understood the power of this positive, 'no-fault' attitude. We focused ahead, and soon the team believed that there was no technical problem we could not solve."

Indirect Communication

Indians will seldom call a spade a spade. Like many Asian cultures, most Indians prefer a more subdued, subtle form of communication, although not to the same degree as the Japanese, Chinese, or Koreans. This indirect communication operates at many levels.

Let's start with the physical. A Westerner new to India is almost always flummoxed by the diversity of head nods. Most Indians shake their heads vigorously left to right a couple of times to signify no. But there are many shades of yes, depending on the region, the speaker, and the context. The Western-style nod, with the head moving up and down, is common only among Indians who are regularly exposed to Western culture. "The South Indian yes can be described as making a figure-eight with one's nose," says Colorado resident and electrical engineer Tim Lenihan, who travels to India on business frequently and is also married to an Indian. A north Indian may indicate encouragement—*Carry on, this makes sense to me*—with a sideways tilt to the left or right; sometimes the tilt is quite jerky and repeated. However, most Westerners mistakenly interpret this as a no.

I recently watched an instrumental performance of Indian sarod maestro Ustad Amjad Ali Khan in Washington, DC. The audience was rapt, as were Khan's two students,

who sat onstage next to him. They indicated their enjoy-
ment by shaking their heads left to right slowly. But most
Americans in the audience first thought that the students
were trying to point to some problem.

Many other head bobs may indicate enthusiasm, sar-
casm, or other emotions. In some cases, you will hear Indians make a sound that almost sounds like a sharp *click*
to indicate no. In north India, some communities indicate
yes with a high-pitched *cheep* made by breathing inward
with the lips almost completely closed. Until you begin to
master these nuances, it is best to confirm the intended
meaning gently, with a broad smile and "Sorry, I didn't understand; how do you mean?"

Going beyond the physical movements and sounds,
an Indian may want to voice a no but tell you yes in an
attempt to preserve your dignity. If you pursue gentle,
polite, but firm questions and listen very carefully along
the way, you will develop the ability to hear conditions,
qualifiers, and other indirect indications that the Indian
is actually trying to tell you no.

In the presence of their boss—or if you *are* their boss
or are much older than them—Indians may tell you yes
because they sense that you want to hear a yes. Disagree-
ing with a superior is considered disrespectful and even
disloyal, particularly in the presence of third parties. If you
have developed trust with the Indians, you may find them
somewhat more open in a one-on-one situation. Another
way to achieve frank dialogue might be to have someone
at the same level or same age as the Indians present, so

he or she may confirm and reconfirm the meaning of the exchange.

When challenged in writing or in a formal situation, Indians may answer yes when they actually mean no, simply to save face or dignity or because they feel cornered. Any sense of victory or satisfaction you feel should be muted until you can confirm that the yes will stick.

Remember that in India, indirectness is not the same as indirection. The former implies subtlety and sophistication; the latter, deceitfulness.

A group of senior American executives and I had two successive meetings with top government officials in New Delhi. The American team was eager for the Indian government to make some changes in policy that would make it easier for Western companies to enter the market. The executive from the Foreign Ministry politely explained the current process to us and then informed us that there was no active proposal to modify the rules; we should plan on bidding for business under the current procedure. He went on to explain candidly the needs and concerns of the Indian government. Next, we met a top official with the ministry that was going to be the beneficiary of these American products. After a number of topics, the issue of policy changes came up again. The response this time was, "Well, please include your suggestions for changes in policy; we will review them appropriately."

On the way back to the hotel, several of the American executives remarked that they were upset with the officials' answers. "We can't be sure who to believe." "They are misleading us with two different stories." One of the visitors told me how he had heard that *India* is an acronym for "I'll Never Do It Again."

I explained that to my bicultural ears, the two officials weren't that far apart—and that they certainly did not intend to mislead or deceive. The first official was giving us the real picture. The second official was merely being polite, as if to say, *You are our guests; if you have an alternative proposal, we won't refuse to receive it.* But there was no promise that it would be acted upon. The message from the officials was clear to me: *We will decide what is right for us, but we won't dismiss you for suggesting that we alter the rules.*

Relationships: *Who* Is More Important than *What*

When first meeting an outsider in a business context, Indians often want to get to know the other person, make connections over mutual interests, and size up the foreigner to see if they will be able to work with him or her. To a foreigner, this may seem like a lot of small talk.

According to Tim Lenihan, "In the West, a lot of emphasis is put on negotiating a solid contract. In India, especially when dealing with medium or small domestic companies, the contract is a guide; personal relationships need to be solid. Larger Indian companies have more experience with the contract concept, but even they want solid relationships with their customers."

In my company, we generally tell our clients to plan a

series of trips to India if they are serious about getting started. Indians will often ask you upon the first meeting, "When will you be back?" If you don't have some acceptable answer to this question, you need to think again before going to India at all.

Lenihan continues, "People have to spend time in India to develop relationships. An afternoon meeting will probably not be enough, especially when a contract needs to be negotiated before you leave the country. It is a good idea to build in extra time for this trust-building, getting-to-know-you process. It may take several trips to close on a contract—and Indians do love to negotiate, so be prepared."

Relationships are built between individuals, not between companies. Thus it's important to keep the same people coming to India so the process doesn't have to be repeated for each neophyte. When Western companies reassign resources too quickly and put someone new in charge of an India initiative, they program themselves for failure. Note that Scott Bayman of General Electric spent fourteen years in India as head of its operations.

Americans tend to think in terms of issues when addressing a problem, while most Indians tend to think in terms of people and emotions. A friend who is a senior executive at a major multinational tells me, "I have been on calls where a cross-geography team is discussing a problem—say, a project that is not progressing well. I will hear the India team say, *Jay is not doing a good job,* or *Ram is not communicating well,* but I hear the US team say, *This is not being done right because we are not following the right process.*" The solution lies in patiently understanding this difference and gradually moving the discussion toward issues, rather than assuming that everyone thinks alike.

When Indian Prime Minister Manmohan Singh announced the appointment of A. K. Antony to lead the Defense Ministry in 2006, most Indians immediately understood the *who* message. Antony is a party stalwart with a clean, no-nonsense, and incorruptible image. Some of the American vendors who hoped to sell weapons to India kept waiting for budgetary projections; such hard financial information, however, is far less important in the Indian context. What was important was that Defense was in the hands of a person who could be trusted to be fair and clean.

Another aspect of Indians' behavior that often confuses visitors is their ability to be very courteous to some and quite brusque with others. Indians can often appear rude to strangers, especially when competing for scarce resources such as a place to sit at a busy airport. But the attitude changes considerably when you move up the hierarchy to being a guest, either of a company or a family. An old Sanskrit saying—*Atithi Devo Bhavah*—equates a guest with God. If you invest time and effort in relationships, Indians will befriend you. Once you move up the hierarchy to a friend, your experience will be similar to Mark Bullard's, who moved from Arkansas in 2007: "I am making good friends in India and finding that friendships here are tighter." In some instances, Indians may start to treat you as family, a virtual brother or sister. If that happens, you are typically accorded the same rights (and responsibilities) as a sibling.

This level of intimacy is not always good in a business context. Mason Byles observes that in India, "Personal friendship frequently is much more important than accountability. If someone is a personal friend but isn't generating the expected results, there is a great reluctance to remove him or her from his or her position in the organization. This is universally true to some extent, but I found the tendency to be much stronger during my time in India than during my non-India career with Hewlett-Packard."

India is notorious for its rules and regulations, but relationships can often trump red tape—as New Yorker Joe Sigelman reports. "In the US, we have developed a whole infrastructure of bureaucracy, and India, funnily enough, is shedding rapidly its bureaucratic inheritance. I think the normal reaction is still bureaucratic, but if you actually develop a personal relationship with somebody, things just get done in real time."

Relationships are two-way streets. When Indians treat you well on your visits over there, there is some expectation of reciprocity when they arrive in your country. Many visiting Indians have told me that they were offended by their business partner's offhand treatment when the Indian partner visited the United States. Small courtesies extended outside office hours to visiting Indians will go a long way in cementing these relationships.

Superstition and Religious Practices

What are considered occult sciences in the West are often mainstream practices in India. Astrology, numerology, and palmistry can affect the functioning of businesses. Some business people won't sign contracts at times or dates deemed inauspicious. Astral charts and priests are often consulted to determine the best time for the inauguration of a factory or office. Astronomical events such as eclipses are generally considered ominous. In times of business or personal crisis, Indians are more inclined to turn to superstitious beliefs, and may stick by the recommendations of their priest, adviser, or fortune-teller.

Even if these expectations seem out of place or silly to you, you may need to adjust some plans. Think what would happen if an Indian wanted to schedule a training session in the United States on Super Bowl Sunday.

Sometimes women behave differently in a work situation than you might expect, but the reason could be tradition. For example, if your top female Indian executive decides to take a backseat during a ceremony inaugurating your new office, don't assume that this has to do with office politics or equality. Many Hindu women don't enter the kitchen or perform certain religious ceremonies during the time that they are menstruating, and they generally don't reveal the reason. Women also consider pregnancy to be a very private matter. You won't see colleagues patting the swollen belly of a co-worker or trying to tell if the baby just kicked. When someone brings a cute baby or bubbly child to an office picnic or other event, you may see a little black dot on his or her forehead. This is to ward off the "evil eye." Indians often believe that excessive praise or adulation is an ill omen. Don't go overboard verbally marveling at the lovely child, especially if you see the parent looking uncomfortable.

Regardless of your religion, you may be invited to some Hindu or Jain temples or Christian churches. A few Hindu temples don't allow non-Hindus; others may require men to enter bare-chested. People of a different religion are generally not allowed inside Muslim mosques or Parsi temples. It is always a good idea to take off your shoes before you enter. Jain temples may have you remove leather belts and wallets. If you are female and you see other women covering their heads, follow suit; it's a good idea for women to keep a large scarf handy in their purses. If any of this makes you uncomfortable, it is always acceptable to decline to participate in a particular activity; no one will mind.

Language

India does *not* have a billion English speakers. In fact, the most sanguine number I have seen applies to English "users," and this may include people whose English vocabulary does not exceed two hundred highly accented and Indianized words. Some reports say that India has 350 million English users and 100 million English speakers. This is still a huge number, but it acknowledges that 90 percent of Indians are not fluent English speakers.

While most business in large Indian companies is conducted in English, Indians have developed their own flavor of the language, with a liberal sprinkling of words taken from Indian languages, and others retained from the English that was spoken a century ago. In addition, certain English words have acquired a special flavor of meaning that may be different from what we expect in the West. Many Indians throw phrases or even sentences from another language into the middle of a thought expressed in English.

Mark Bullard notes, "English is different here. After you adopt some of the local terminology, it becomes easier to communicate. It is good to learn a little bit of Hindi. Any attempt to use Hindi is always welcomed, even if you screw it up."

An Indian may refer to a spare tire as a "stepney"—after the town in Wales where automotive components were manufactured a century ago. When Indians refer to a "scheme," it simply denotes a plan, nothing nefarious or evil. If they remark that they will "intimate" you, it's nothing passionate; it simply means that they will inform you. If their firm is in a "tie-up" with another company, they have an alliance of some kind.

Indians count in lakhs and crores rather than millions and billions. One lakh (or lac) refers to 100,000, written in Indian English as 1,00,000. One crore is 10 million, written as 1,00,00,000. I also recommend care in referring to calendar dates in India; it is better to write out June 3, 2008, because an Indian will write it is 3/6/2008, whereas an

American may write it as 6/3/2008. Some Indian sources use military time: 1300 hours, instead of 1:00 PM.

When you are new to India, it is important that you speak slowly and enunciate your words carefully. Your accent may be strange to Indian ears, and by slowing down you give them a chance to keep up and process the information. Remember that many Indians are too polite to interrupt you or to ask for clarification if they don't understand a particular word or phrase. It is also a good idea to pause briefly between paragraphs as you speak to let the meaning sink in. In turn, it is perfectly normal to ask your Indian counterpart to slow down and to repeat or clarify something you don't understand.

Avoid the use of metaphors and idioms, especially sports idioms. Indians don't play baseball, so when you want to hit a home run with your sales, they may be befuddled. One of my clients asked an art vendor to add some five o'clock shadow to a video game character's face and was met with puzzlement.

Break down long or complex sentences into simpler sentences to reduce the possibility of misunderstanding. Also, avoid contractions. To the Indian ear, the way Americans pronounce *can't* sounds like *can.* To avoid confusion, substitute *cannot.* Assume difference, not agreement. Repeat key thoughts. And finally, have the other party summarize what they understood, in their own words, where possible.

ROOM SERVICE

Joe Sigelman recalls how misunderstanding can have unintended consequences. "There was one day when I had forgotten to eat the whole day and it was now 1:00 AM. This was a few months after I had first arrived in India. I remember trying to figure out where in Chennai I could get sanitary food after midnight. I remembered that I could get room service from my hotel, which was around the corner from our first office, and have it sent over. So I called over Ashok, our office assistant. I told him that I had ordered a large package of food for myself and a few of my colleagues. I asked him if he would do me a favor and walk over and collect the room service for me.

"He nodded vigorously and strode off. About forty-five minutes later, I was giving a speech to the night shift and wondered where my food was—the walk is just two minutes. All of a sudden, out of the corner of my eye, I saw Ashok coming into the office carrying a giant suitcase on his head, sweating, dragging his feet. I instantly thought that the hotel must have sent over place settings or something grand, as I had been staying there for some time already. *Wow,* I thought, *what great service.*

"I finished my speech and walked toward my office. As I approached, I noticed the suitcase looked familiar. Then I got closer and realized it was my own suitcase. I opened it and saw my underwear and other belongings! He had packed my whole room! I turned to Ashok, perplexed. He responded with an eager smile: 'Sir, are you liking my room service?' How do you ask this lovely man to take my luggage back, unpack it, and bring me my dinner?"

Appearance and Manners

Indians are relaxed about dress. Men from overseas can wear suits, sport coats, or just shirts and slacks depending on the industry and the weather. For women, I recommend conservative midlength skirts or pantsuits; avoid sleeveless or low-cut tops. Guy Rabbat recalls an occasion when a senior American female executive wore a somewhat low-cut blouse to a business meeting and the Indian men in the room became quite uncomfortable, not knowing where to look as they spoke to her.

Leisure suits attract sniggers in the United States, but weather and local practice make it quite acceptable for Indian men to wear "safari suits"—as they are called in-country. Sikh men almost always wear turbans, since their religion prohibits them from cutting their hair. You may see some traditional Muslims wearing caps and long beards.

In old-style companies and rural areas, businessmen may wear a traditional dhoti-kurta. This attire is accepted as formal wear; it is equivalent to a suit and tie in clubs that have dress codes. Indian politicians are often seen wearing dhoti-kurta. A dhoti is a rectangular piece of broadcloth, often white, that is draped around the legs to look like baggy trousers; Western sources sometimes describe it as a loincloth, but that word is culturally loaded and I don't recommend you use it. A kurta is a long shirt that may or may not have a collar.

Women in India may come to work in Western clothing, particularly in Mumbai. More often than not, however, you will see Indian women wearing traditional sarees, or salwar-kameez, at work. A dash or streak of red color in a woman's hair indicates that she is married. Married or single women may wear a colored dot, or bindi, on their foreheads, but you won't see a widow with a bindi. Be aware that nose rings and earrings are ancient Indian traditions, not an import of modern Western body-piercing practices. You won't encounter tongue studs or navel rings much.

At weddings in north India, the bride wears a brightly colored saree, usually with a lot of red. The bridegroom (and the word is almost never shortened to *groom*) may wear Western or Indian clothes. If you attend a funeral in India, you may see many people dressed in white clothes, since white, not black, is the Hindu color of mourning.

In most urban settings in modern India, you may greet both men and women with a handshake. "Sometimes shaking hands in India feels like holding a wet fish," jokes Tim Lenihan. He goes on to conjecture, "Strong handshaking can be thought of as being very aggressive in a culture that seeks peace and harmony."

If you are going to spend more than a day in India, learn how to voice the word *namaste* with your palms together and, if possible, your head slightly bowed. *Namaste* (or *namaskar*) is used as a greeting at the beginning or the end of a meeting and will work throughout most parts of India. This single gesture disarms most Indians and earns you advance forgiveness for a dozen faux pas.

You may see Indians of all ages bending down to touch the feet of an elder or respected teacher as a mark of respect. As a foreigner, you are not expected to practice this Indian rite. However, an Indian child might touch your feet if you attend a special occasion or ceremony.

It is uncommon to see cross-gender physical contact, such as hugging or kissing, in a work setting in India. However, American men new to India should be cautioned that Indian males are quite comfortable with same-gender contact. If an Indian man puts his hand on your shoulder or gives you an unusually long handshake, it simply conveys that he is getting more comfortable with you, even as you squirm!

Regardless of gender, Indians stand much closer to one another in crowds and elevators than Americans and most Europeans are used to. The lack of interpersonal distance can be uncomfortable at first. Says Mark Bullard, "Indians are generally very nice people. The exceptions to this rule are traffic, queues, and elevators. Your comfort zone will be violated in all instances. Embrace it and move on; it's simply the way it is." On a related point, note that the use of deodorant is not as widespread in India. That, together with the heat, often results in smell that creates discomfort in the minds of American visitors.

As you spend time with Indians, you may observe that they often make snap judgments about other Indians' social class based on their clothing and their manner of walking and talking. For example, you might see your Indian host act directive and short with someone of perceived lower status even if he or she just met this individual. This does mean that the Indian is angry or upset. In fact, in the very next breath your host may continue to be very deferential and courteous to you or to another colleague.

Names

> *James Bond lands in Chennai and introduces himself.*
> *"Good day, the name is Bond, James Bond."*
> *"Good day, the name is Murthy. Srinivas Murthy. K. V. Srinivasa Murthy. Kumarappa Vellore Srinivasa Murthy. Welcome to Chennai."*

Indian names can be confusing. In north India, most names are structured with the first name (often called the given or Christian name or forename) first, followed by the last name (often called the surname or second name). In some cases, especially in Gujarat and Maharashtra, a male's middle name is taken from his father's first name. In south India, however, the last name may appear first and the given name, last. So it would be wrong to address Srinivasa Gopal as Srinivasa (which might actually be his father's name); you want to call him Gopal. As in many other facets of Indian life, it is best to ask how someone prefers to be addressed.

Indians will seldom address someone in higher authority or someone far senior to them in age by their first name. If an Indian takes you home to meet his or her parents or grandparents, it is proper to address them as *Mr. Last Name* or *Mrs. Last Name,* rather than using their first names. Sometimes an additional honorific is added to indicate special position. In other cases, the suffix *-ji* may be added to a person's name as a more respectful way of addressing them. So while a revered teacher might be called Guru-ji, a senior scientist might be addressed only as Dr. Verma, and a community leader could be addressed with an honorific such as *sahib* added to the end of the name. For example, the appropriate way to address musical maestro Ravi Shankar is Shankar Sahib. Indians will forgive you the first few times if you address someone the wrong way.

Negotiations

> *Question: How many Indians does it take to have three divergent opinions at the table?*
> *Answer: Just two.*

By applying the lessons from earlier sections of this chapter during any interactions with Indian counterparts, you stand a better chance of understanding and being understood. However, be ready for further frustration as you negotiate agreements.

When it began operations in India, a major Western company that presently sells hundreds of millions of dollars of product into the country was taken aback because its customer summarily rejected an eighty-page contract. The Indian side wanted a very simple agreement with the key conditions laid out and an assumption that *We will work the rest out as we go.* Lawyers for the Western company were accustomed to spelling out almost every possible contingency and a related course of action and felt quite uncomfortable with such a fuzzy approach. Officials with the Indian customer reacted quite negatively to their suggestions, taking this to imply that the vendor did not trust them. Negotiations dragged on for more than a year. When I spoke to the Western company a few weeks after the Indian side apparently gave in on most of the fine print, I cautioned that this might not be a durable agreement. Sure enough, the vendor encountered difficulties in converting the agreement into a trusting relationship a few months later.

There is much scholarly research on cross-cultural negotiation involving American, European, and Japanese participants. But little of it applies directly to Indians, and there is a dearth of current academic material on the Indian mind-set. Given the polycultural nature of Indian society, there's also a debate about whether an "Indian mind-set" even exists.

Dr. Rajesh Kumar, formerly director of the Indian Research Center at the Aarhus School of Business in Denmark, provides a framework for understanding Indian negotiating behavior. Western negotiators tend to focus primarily on the behavior of the Indian partner. Kumar advises us to look beyond behavior to the underlying worldview—the lens through which an Indian may view the negotiation.

First is what Kumar calls brahmanical idealism, which he describes as an "introverted form of thinking" where "external reality is rationalized rather than dealt with very directly in a pragmatic, hands-on way." This tendency drives Indians to seek a perfect solution, even if it takes more time than others may think reasonable.

Layered over this idealism and often running at cross purposes with it is what Kumar terms anarchical individualism. Such individualism is not typical in Asian countries such as Japan and Korea. Indian individuals act out their personal views unconditionally and may find it difficult to mutually coordinate action for shared outcomes. Interplay between idealism and individualism causes discussions to drag on seemingly interminably; it may also bring high emotions and repeated unpredictability to bear on complex negotiations, according to Kumar.

I am a practitioner and not a scholar, but I can confirm that my anecdotal experience is generally consistent with Kumar's theories. Sometimes Indians want to discuss and argue as an end in itself. The negotiated agreements might not be much affected by these vigorous discussions over lunch or dinner. Westerners, Americans in particular, are well advised to let discussions play out fully. Forcing an agreement too quickly is likely to cost you in the long term. I remind my clients that it was no coincidence that a Nobel Prize–winning economist chose the title *The Argumentative Indian* for his book of essays.

I also encourage outsiders to not give up too early in any important negotiations with Indian vendors or customers. Once initial sincerity and interest are well established, it is also a mistake to jump to the conclusion that the other side is being duplicitous, deceitful, or opaque. In fact, in my experience a skillful, sincere cross-cultural negotiator can often encourage the Indian side to be more open than you might reasonably expect.

Don Hollis, the former Deluxe Corporation executive, recommends that you leverage strong on-the-ground consultants and analysts when developing the specifications for a development or service project. He also advises a comprehensive and specific feedback loop between the buying organization and the consultants prior to having them relay the requirements to Indian partners. I agree with Hollis's advice, both when your company is new to India and when you have an executive who is new to the nation, even if your company is long established there.

Conclusion

Almost everything that happens in India has an explanation in an Indian context. It is not better or worse—it is Indian. Says Tim Lenihan, "Will it change? Perhaps, when Indians want it to change. Can foreigners change it? Not likely. With exposure comes understanding. You may not agree, but you should be tolerant."

The bottom line is that managers who actively step out of the comfort zone of their surroundings to make time and friends will prosper in India. Those who don't will likely limit their success.

CHAPTER 4

Human Resources

While many aspects of India are confusing to an executive new to the country, nothing is potentially more so than decisions around human resources. Myths and paradoxes proliferate. Let me list a few that you might hear in Western circles:

- Indians may be good technically, but you can't trust them to manage or lead.
- India is too expensive; you should look at country X, Y, or Z instead.
- It's impossible to trust the quality of manufacturing or service by Indian workers.
- India speaks English; you will have no trouble expanding your business there.
- There is a *shortage* of manpower in India, which will stifle its growth.
- There is an *excess* of manpower in India; unemployed and disenchanted voters may cause political unrest.

There is a smidgeon of truth in each statement, but as sweeping generalizations, each of these statements can lead you down the wrong path. If you have heard these myths, here are some facts that may lead you to reconsider.

Arun Sarin was appointed CEO of UK-based Vodafone, where he manages thirty thousand employees and annual revenues of about $50 billion. Sarin is a graduate of the Indian Institute of Technology Kharagpur. Indra Nooyi rose to become the CEO of PepsiCo, one of the most valuable companies in the world, and she leads 170,000 employees. Nooyi is a native of Chennai and a graduate of the Indian Institute of Management Calcutta. According to Scott Bayman, who led General Electric's operation in India for fourteen years, "Indian managers travel well, maybe better than most other nationals." GE has transferred or promoted several hundred executives first hired in India to locations in other countries. As we will see later in this chapter, Citigroup's experience with managers from India is similar. Home-grown Indian executives run virtually all Indian companies, with the possible exception of the aviation industry. Home-grown executives also run many Indian subsidiaries of American companies. Many Indian managers are excellent leaders.

Imagine that you spend three days at the Hilton Hotel at Nariman Point in south Mumbai interviewing candidates (screened by a top search firm) to lead your consumer goods business in India. When you ask about the salaries and benefits, you may find that these local candidates are compensated on par with American standards. However, this is not the norm. The vast majority of Indian employees whom you hire today are not compensated nearly as well. In fact, in my consulting, I sometimes find that Western companies take advantage of the lower Indian salaries to the point that they hire too many people for too few tasks. If you do your homework, locate in the right city, and hire the right leaders, your people costs will stay attractive for many years.

Until 1991, a protected domestic market and over-whelming regulations discouraged high-quality manufac-turing and innovation. In today's India, whole sectors have been transformed by deregulation and competition and are operating at near-world-class levels. Automotive ven-dors run lean manufacturing at "Six-Sigma" standards. The top hospitals have metrics that match American quality. The best hotels offer extravagant service. Airlines such as Jet Airways and Kingfisher offer in-flight service levels not seen in the United States for twenty years.

There are twenty-three official languages in India and dozens of dialects. You may find that in Kannada-speaking Bangalore, the majority of your factory workers are actu-ally more comfortable speaking Tamil, the language of the neighboring state. In Mumbai, where the local language is Marathi, your door-to-door salespeople may need to be more fluent in Gujarati. When you do read English written by the average college graduate in India, you may find the grammar, word choice, and style to be a significant hin-drance to understanding at first. While English is the written language in which much of India conducts business, it is important to understand the regional nuances, the needs of your Indian customers, and the requirements of interacting with the corporate headquarters in the West.

Because the economy has grown so rapidly, there is undoubtedly a shortage of qualified and experienced managers. In certain skills and at certain experience levels, demand has skyrocketed while supply can only increase linearly, so you will find few qualified and available candidates. If you need someone with twenty years of semiconductor chip design experience, don't be surprised if you can't find many takers, since twenty years ago there wasn't much chip design going on in India. If you need college graduates, clerical staff, or factory laborers, however, there are vast quantities of willing workers. Companies that outsource high-end video game art to India find that vendors are able to train hundreds of employees who have master's degrees in fine arts to understand how to use the latest software and work under the guidance of a Western-trained art director fairly readily. For many jobs performed by employees with high school diplomas in the United States, you can hire smart and willing college grads in India. At one ultramodern factory near Mumbai, I was told that all the machine tool operators had bachelor's degrees.

The HR Function

For a business of any size to be successful in twenty-first-century India, you must build a strong and flexible human resource department compared with operations in most emerging countries. Trained HR professionals are readily available, although they are certainly well compensated. You may also find some traditional personnel managers who think of themselves as payroll supervisors and benefits trackers rather than curators of talent. Pick your HR leadership very carefully when you start out in India.

You can seldom transplant Western HR processes into India without substantial localization. Hiring, benefits, promotions, and separation procedures generally need fine-tuning. Expatriate and repatriation policies must be adjusted to account for special considerations in India.

From the West, you might bring in diversity training, sexual harassment policies, practices relating to compliance with Sarbanes-Oxley and the Foreign Corrupt Practices Act, and other laws and practices specific to your industry and your company.

I asked Bala Vasireddi, who runs US Internetworking, Inc., operations in India for AT&T, about the kinds of problems he has observed in other global teams. "Too often, management teams in India tend to place undue reliance on process to accomplish things. What they miss is the ability to constantly monitor if the process is serving its purpose, and if not, to retool it. Such inflexible processes exist in many companies and determine crucial functions like recruiting, performance appraisals, salary hikes, et cetera." This risks creating a situation in which the offshore center is unable to deliver on its business objectives. Processes become out of tune with deliverables, and things start falling apart.

Recruiting

In India, entry-level staffers are often recruited on college campuses. Most colleges have active placement departments. Web sites that focus on recruitment are led by Naukri.com (*naukri* means "job" in Hindi). Monster.com and the *Times of India* are other popular locations for job postings at all levels. Free Web sites such as Craigslist aren't very popular in India as of this writing.

Salaries are no secret in India. Junior employees will share their salaries, raises, and reviews with their peers. Avinash Agarwal, who built and ran Sun Microsystems' India development center, jokes, "It is not just the employees who tell each other. It is one employee's mother gossiping with another worker's aunt. One of the first things people ask you when you tell them that you have a new job is, 'What is your new salary?'"

Regardless of your industry or specialty, when you recruit junior employees in India, you are going to compete with the largest information technology employers. That's because Indian companies led by Tata Consultancy Services (TCS) and American companies led by IBM and Accenture hire in such large numbers and across so many skill sets. In 2007, the top five Indian companies collectively hired more than a hundred thousand new employees, mostly at junior levels. In this environment, start-ups and smaller companies find it hard just to get attention from young candidates.

Cleartrip.com, a travel start-up funded by Silicon Valley venture capital firm Kleiner Perkins, faced this problem in Mumbai. "We have managed to create an energetic and innovative brand. Through this approach, we offer an alternative to the larger employers and attract the mavericks who truly want to work on projects where they have a direct and relevant impact at an early stage in their careers," says co-founder Stuart Crighton.

Display ads for senior positions often appear in the print version of leading newspapers and business magazines. Some entry-level positions may also be advertised on billboards in major cities.

Many retained search firms from the West have followed their clients into India and are doing very well in top-level searches. For example, Korn/Ferry International, Stanton Chase, and Egon Zehnder are well known in India. Long-established domestic firms such as ABC Consultants have offices in most major cities. Similar to the West, there are also hundreds of small contingency search firms, many of which are specialized in some way.

Education

In recent years, Western media has highlighted the role of India's top educational institutions in shaping its economy. In 2007, the seven Indian Institutes of Technology (IITs) accepted 4,193 undergraduate students out of 300,000 applicants, a selection ratio of 1.4 percent. The six Indian Institutes of Management (IIMs) accepted 1,490 students for their graduate programs in business out of 191,000 applicants; that is a selection ratio of 0.7 percent. By contrast, the top Ivy League schools in the United States typically accept 9 to 15 percent of applicants. Add relatively lavish budgets and a dedicated faculty, and it's not surprising that these students are hot commodities in the job market long before they graduate. But that is exactly the problem: There are not enough IIT and IIM graduates to go around. You will need to reach beyond these elite schools to hire most of your employees.

There are dozens of other great universities and colleges with well-established reputations. These include the Birla Institute of Technology and Science in Pilani, St. Stephens College in Delhi, Madras Christian College in Chennai, the University Department of Chemical Technology in Mumbai, the Indian Institute of Science in Bangalore, the National Institute of Design in Ahmedabad, and many others. Inquire locally if you are not sure about the reputation of an institution.

Quality begins to get spotty once you reach farther into universities that aren't so well known. Still, you may find some excellent employees from B-grade institutions, so don't dismiss candidates solely based on the source of their education.

Another source of qualified graduates is students returning from overseas. India's growing upper middle class can now afford to send their children overseas for college. In fact, more than seventy thousand students from India attend college in the United States alone, more than from any other country. Tens of thousands of additional Indian students travel to Canada, Australia, the United Kingdom, and other countries to obtain their degrees. In decades past, India worried about the so-called brain drain in which the brightest minds left the country and never returned. This trend has now been reversed. Today, an increasing number of Indians working overseas are returning to their homeland, attracted by its growing economy and a chance to boost career prospects—a phenomenon referred to as the brain gain.

That's the good news. Now for the bad.

While government-funded elementary and secondary schooling is generally affordable for most Indians, it is often necessary for parents to supplement it with expensive private tutoring or coaching. If they can afford it, many Indians prefer to send their children to private elementary and secondary schools. At the college level, there is a dire shortage of good government-funded alternatives; private institutions have started to flourish, many of which have sprung up since liberalization began. The quality of these private entities can be world-class, such as the Hyderabad's Indian School of Business or Gandhinagar's Dhirubhai Ambani Institute of Information and Communication Technology. But it can also be abysmal. At other colleges, overcrowded classrooms, inadequate labs, underqualified teachers, and corrupt officials are unfortunately not uncommon.

India today has 68 percent literacy, and every year several hundred thousand Indians graduate from college. However, only 15 percent of these graduates are employable in occupations that require a college degree. "So it is a sad state of affairs when the guy who drives my car for me is also a graduate of some college," bemoans Sandeep Chaudhary, a practice leader at Hewitt Associates.

Joe Sigelman, founder of OfficeTiger, now part of RR Donnelley, agrees that government has failed to keep up with the needs in education. In response to the dearth of public education, the private sector is investing in on-the-job training for its employees. "Education has fallen to the companies. It is a necessary and substantial investment," laments Sigelman. Most midsize to large employers find it necessary to train fresh recruits for four to forty weeks, depending on the job. Lonnie Sapp, OfficeTiger's former chief operating officer, recalls, "During the forming years of OfficeTiger, it was painfully clear that our fresh recruits lacked experience and exposure. Therefore, we focused our attention on setting up a robust training department that utilized a continuous learning approach based on real-life business scenarios and Western management practices. If something did go wrong with client delivery, we would take it back into the classroom and make certain the individuals involved understood what they did wrong and teach them how to do it correctly. This approach worked well, and the training department continued to grow and develop as a result of the department taking on a life of its own and adjusting to local learning styles." Sapp also notes that a simple way to build trust and confidence is to have employees repeat what you just said when you doubt they understood the command or request.

For many impoverished Indians, a good education is the path for their children to lead a dramatically better life than their own. It is not unusual to find a lower-middle-class Indian family spending a third or more of their household income on the college education of a child. It is also not unusual to find a twenty-four-year-old college graduate whose compensation exceeds that of both his blue-collar parents put together. On a related note, when you hire an Indian employee, you need to be aware that he or she may be supporting not only a spouse and children but also the education of his or her siblings, and perhaps the maintenance of retired parents.

White-Collar Workers

Junior Levels

At the junior levels in India, there is an abundance of applicants for any job. Clerical, customer service, telemarketing, and warehousing positions are normally filled by high school graduates in the West. But such openings will often attract candidates with bachelor's degrees in India. Alok Sethi, who runs Franklin Templeton's India back-end operations, cautions Western companies against recruiting overqualified individuals for jobs that don't require brilliance. "Labor is relatively inexpensive; you may be able to recruit an associate for five or six thousand dollars a year." But "will this person stay? Will he or she find the job fulfilling?"

When recruiting for entry-level positions, it is typical for Indian companies to put interviewees through a battery of tests and/or conduct group discussions with multiple candidates in the same room. This may be followed by a small panel of interviewers from the employer speaking with candidates who pass the first round. For the top- and middle-tier colleges, these processes are performed on campus many months ahead of graduation.

Candidates who accept an offer may change their minds and feel too embarrassed to inform the employer, who only finds out when the employee does not report in on the appointed date and time. Experienced employers often issue more appointment letters than they have open positions, in anticipation of such attrition. According to Avinash Agarwal, formerly at Sun India, "A recruiter in Bangalore once told me that the average midlevel engineer may accept two or three job offers simultaneously."

Neither law nor common practice in India prohibits asking about age, religion, gender, parents, family, caste, social background, and other questions that make the average American executive cringe. Your own company practices or your personal sensibilities might limit you from asking such questions, but you may find that candidates routinely list the information on résumés. Job ads commonly place age limits on certain positions.

Many entry-level workers continue to live with their families or with relatives. Door-to-door transportation by bus or SUV is an expected benefit from most well-known companies, except in cities and neighborhoods that are well served by commuter trains, such as Mumbai and Delhi. Some employees may ride motorcycles or bicycles into the office as their primary transportation. Another expected benefit is lunch and snacks provided in-house. Fortunately, there are third-party providers that can package these services at very reasonable prices.

If entry-level workers live in their own apartments or even share one with friends, the cost of accommodations makes a big dent in their disposable income. For this reason, many young professionals who move from the eastern states of Bihar, West Bengal, Orissa, and Jharkhand to prosperous Mumbai in the west or Delhi in the north will readily move back closer to home and accept *lower* salaries for the comfort of proximity to family and rent-free accommodations.

One way to attract and retain employees is by successfully branding your company. American or European companies that happen to be well known in India have an automatic advantage. But start-ups and lesser-known foreign companies face a challenge with not only the potential employee but also the circle of influence that includes the parents, spouse, friends, neighbors, and—for young employees—prospective spouses and in-laws.

Vin Dham, inventor of the Intel's Pentium chip and now a venture investor, recounts a story about serenading a desirable recruit for Pune-based Nevis Network. "I was visiting and the head of the India branch asked me for help in recruiting a prospective employee who was very talented and desirable. I met the engineer, and he was quite excited about coming to work at Nevis, but also had an offer from Intel. He was engaged to be married, and he was concerned that his father-in-law-to-be knew all about Intel but had never heard of Nevis! So I then spoke to the father-in-law, told him who I was and why our little company was so exciting. Finally, with the blessing of his father-in-law, the young man joined us."

Midlevel Employees

India's rapid economic growth has resulted in the creation of many midlevel positions in many industries where few existed before. But because historically companies have not built nonmanagement career tracks, midlevel employees feel that their expanded responsibilities should include supervisory roles, whether their personality or maturity warrants it or not. Thus, it is important to be explicit about what exactly a job will entail, perhaps even addressing whether or not it will involve management responsibilities and explaining why or why not.

When you make an offer to a midlevel employee working at another company, don't expect him or her to report to work in two weeks. Most companies require notice periods of one or two months, at times even more. You may want to offer to buy out the notice period as a kind of signing bonus if you are in a hurry for the new employee to start. This is not uncommon.

Historically, many companies in India offered liberal

benefits packages such as car loans, housing loans, rental reimbursement, an allowance for car and driver, and more. India's tax rules made it advantageous to offer such non-cash compensation, which could account for up to a third or more of total compensation. One major American company that I know structures its compensation as 40 percent base, 12 percent retirement, with the remaining 48 percent in a basket of benefits; employees can choose the one most appropriate to them.

Nowadays, though, some of these benefits are less attractive to employees. The reasons are twofold. The Central Government imposed a new "fringe benefits tax," which discourages the use of such benefits. And according to Hewitt's Chaudhary, the average age of managers has shifted from the forties to the twenty-five-to-thirty-five age bracket; thus some of those traditional benefits, such as kids' education and retirement ("superannuation"), are valued less. More and more, companies are starting to pay cash in lieu of benefits.

There is a myth that large multinationals like Accenture and IBM, which are growing rapidly in India, tend to overpay for talent. While getting started, such companies might overpay temporarily, but they tend to normalize their salary structures very quickly. Four years in, they are definitely not overpaying anymore. In fact, the well-respected brands in India, as in most other countries, can get away with paying a bit less than their peers.

Salary Increases and Retention

In any buoyant free-market economy, jobs for the experienced are plentiful, salaries start to rise, people begin to switch jobs more often, and attrition starts to become a problem. But although Hewitt Associates surveys highlight that India has seen the fastest rise in salaries of any country for several years, there are three factors that you should note. First of all, a few years ago salaries for individual employees in India were rising at 20 to 25 percent per year—but since 2004, the increase has been pretty steady at 14 to 15 percent annually. Second, these increases are from very low base levels. Third, since so much of the high-volume hiring is at the entry level, *median* salaries have actually dipped in the most recent year. As of this writing, Hewitt predicts that average salary increases for the next two years will be in the range of 13 to 15 percent annually.

In India, more and more, part of an employee's total compensation is contingent on performance. This applies to all level of management, down to the clerical and support level. Performance-based pay now constitutes 10 to 20 percent of a middle manager's salary. For a top executive, that figure rises to 25 to 35 percent.

To control costs and manage retention, companies are rapidly taking to the second- and third-tier cities where both salary and real estate costs are much lower. Hewitt Associates sees expansion in Trivandrum, Cochin, Coimbatore, and Pune. HSBC has a center in Vizag, Genpact is expanding in Jaipur, Dell in Chandigarh. OfficeTiger opened a satellite center in Trivandrum for both redundancy and retention reasons.

Pawan Goenka, president of the automotive sector of the $5 billion Mahindra & Mahindra groups, explains that their attrition rate is 13 to 14 percent, which is in line with most equitable companies. "We are very concerned about employee engagement and spend a lot of senior management time on it. Pay also is increasing rapidly. Our top 10 percent employees have doubled their pay in three years."

Average employee attrition rates of 15 to 20 percent are not uncommon at well-respected companies. But it pays to look a little deeper. Joe Sigelman used to receive a daily report on every employee who left and the reason why. He found that averages masked the problem. Some managers had near zero attrition, whereas a few saw more than half their reports leave in a given year. "Companies have to realize that when there is attrition, we should look at our own navels. It is not primarily the result of market forces, wherein one company across the street in those crammed techno parks is offering a few rupees more each month. It is actually a result of a lack of good management." Sigelman responded by offering training and coaching to managers who were marginal. A few managers who proved unresponsive or incapable of their roles were removed.

Another senior executive in the United States agrees: "My company's subsidiary in India was facing 45 percent overall attrition, but my particular group had zero attrition. Everything else was the same—only the immediate management was different. High employee turnover in a multicultural, global team can be the result of a poor boss located in India or in the West."At the start-up Cleartrip, the founders have addressed this issue by investing in "teamship," organizing off-site activities from white-water rafting to interdepartment cricket games to build camaraderie. The onus for deciding and executing these activities is on a rotating staff committee of the departments themselves.

Another potential cause for turnover may be miscommunication between managers and employees. Sometimes, managers in India tend to avoid conflict and defer negative feedback, which can deprive employees of the opportunity to improve themselves. Then, when employees do get a less-than-rosy review, they are disappointed and ready to accept the first tolerable offer that gets them out of the clutches of the bad manager. On the other hand, Americans can be perceived as overly nice and polite. When an American raves to Indian counterparts or subordinates, "Wow, excellent. Great job," the Indian employees might misread the praise and begin to imagine themselves superlative performers—only to be later disappointed when they do not receive that 5-on-a-scale-of-5 rating. My advice is to be measured in your praise and to consider giving both negative and positive feedback.

Layoffs and Separations

In India, there are two categories of employees: workers and managerial employees. It is difficult to lay off workers, but managers can be asked to leave with very short notice, and they have little recourse. In most cases, nei-ther the employee nor the employer wants an involuntary separation on the record. So when laying off or firing em-ployees, companies often tell them that their job is going away; they can either accept a severance package or be fired. Confides an industry insider, "The market being so hot, I have never had a single person decline the offer. Not only do they get to keep the separation package, most of them find new jobs within days. And they also show up in personnel records as having left voluntarily, as opposed to having been fired."

Productivity

Before you can address productivity issues, you need to know what you are up against, which is why I generally encourage clients to track productivity of all Indian work-ers, whether they are employees or vendor personnel.

In fields such as chip design, some American companies report that Indian workers achieve about 70 percent of Western productivity levels. At an electronics manufac-turer, the country head told me that his engineers were at about 80 percent of American productivity levels on an hour-by-hour basis, but because they worked longer hours, they were actually able to achieve productivity parity on a month-by-month basis. Joe Sigelman asserts that by good training and management, OfficeTiger brought its Indian employees to productivity parity within twelve months of starting a new process. Guy Rabbat has seen a significant improvement in engineer productivity in India since the days when he was a board member at General Electric and a top executive for Wipro-GE. "Today, Indian engineers are highly capable and can manage entire projects by themselves."

When you have an initiative that is owned in the West, with some people in India working on it, it is wise to expect that the Indian team will be less productive initially. If the initiative is owned in India, however, it's wise to assume the reverse. Making such distributed teams work effectively requires considerable personal sacrifices for managers and employees. Work–life balance is often disrupted in significant ways. You work all day in your time zone, and then you work with the team on the other side of the world in the evening. You are up all night trying to resolve issues in India, then you turn around and go to the office for meetings the next morning. Often, companies are not yet mature enough to provide an infrastructure that facilitates cooperation among co-workers. The result can be resentment on both sides. I have not seen any magic-bullet solutions to such situations. But it is important for top executives and HR professionals to recognize that such situations exist and allow operational leaders to propose ways to cope with them. I face such a pressure-cooker work style myself; my own solution is to take frequent short vacations.

CITIGROUP INDIA

One of the great American success stories in India is Citi-group, with more than twenty-two thousand employees in units that include retail banking, consumer finance, venture capital, and a global capital markets entity for the Indian market, as well as a large offshoring operation that serves Citi worldwide. In other chapters, we will look at Citi's market success. Here we will simply examine some of the company's human resource approaches.

Citigroup India CEO Sanjay Nayar attributes much of his operation's success to its regional talent management. He says, "We have been able to leverage the human capital advantage well enough, and quite ahead of the curve." Indeed, Citi was a pioneer in the development of business process outsourcing operations in India. Citi also leveraged the Indian information technology competitive advantage by setting up a captive IT offshoring unit called Citigroup Information Technology Offshoring Services (CITOS). Additionally, the abundance of highly talented management graduates in India enabled the bank to create a knowledge process offshoring unit. This special division, consisting of about five hundred highly skilled professionals, supports international investment banking teams as they develop industry ideas and client pitches. Such initiatives have been critical to Citigroup's success in India.

Citi also offers international careers to its promising India managers. In fact, more than three hundred Indian employees have moved on to positions outside the country. The most prominent example is Ajay Banga, who heads the global consumer group at Citi International in New York. If your company can offer global mobility to young professionals, you'll have a leg up on the competition.

As the quality of talent in India has risen over the last several years, Citi's dependence on sourcing talent imported from the United States has dramatically dropped. The strength of the Indian operations has been its local knowledge of its top management. There are a few expatriate employees in India at senior levels, but not necessarily Americans. All employees from middle management on down are Indian, with strong local market knowledge.

When I asked Nayar about managers from overseas relocating to India, he replied, "The clear marker of success in India is to be able to work with its people coming from diverse backgrounds. To gain the confidence and respect of the people who work for you is very important. Understanding markets and clients is also equally challenging."

Blue-Collar Workers

Labor-unit costs are extremely low across India. But labor productivity can vary dramatically from region to region—and in many cases, from company to company in the same region. Receptivity to employers can also vary by geography. If you will be employing a few thousand factory workers, labor conditions should be a major consideration when setting up shop, probably as important a factor in determining your plant location as are availability of electric power and proximity to material resources and transportation.

Trade unions in India are usually aligned to specific political parties rather than to individual trades such as machinist or truck driver. For example, the three million members of the Centre of Indian Trade Unions (CITU) are allied with the Communist Party of India (Marxist). The International Trade Union Congress (INTUC) is allied with the Congress Party. In Mumbai, you may encounter the Shiv Sena–allied Bharatiya Kamgar Sena (Indian Worker Army). The Bharatiya Mazdoor Sangh (Indian Labor Union) is allied to the Bharatiya Janata Party, which claims to be the largest trade union in the country with about eight million members.

Unions are no longer a major worry for employers. Employee strikes and employer-initiated lockouts in the private sector have diminished significantly in recent years, partly as a result of improving work conditions and wages. From January through September 2006, there were 154 strikes and 192 lockouts across the country, which resulted in the loss of 3.16 million man-days and 10.6 million man-days, respectively, according to the Indian government's most recent economic survey. This was 4.4 percent lower than the previous year and substantially lower than the 540 strikes in 1999.

Many laws pertaining to blue-collar workers in India apply to companies above a certain head count. The specific number varies depending on the particular law. It is not unusual to see Indian entrepreneurs set up multiple corporations, partly to stay below the trigger limits on such laws.

At most modern Indian companies, worker productivity is rising rapidly. According to Pawan Goenka, Mahindra & Mahindra has improved shop-floor productivity by a factor of two in the last seven years.

Indian manufacturing is expanding, and Hewitt Associates expects it to start booming by 2010. Compared with China, India consumes a lot of what it manufactures—something like 85 percent. While costs in India are 15 to 20 percent higher than China, it is primarily due to scale, according to Hewitt's Chaudhary.

Conclusion

India's biggest asset is its human potential, *if* you know how to use it. While there are challenges in finding and retaining good employees, Western companies can generally do quite well. You would be wise to offer international careers to your most promising India employees; in a few years, you may find that Western employees are eager to add a stint in India to their careers.

CHAPTER 5

Marketing in India

When sales of washing machines began accelerating in India, the local Unilever operation, which had already had a long track record of successes, began R&D for a detergent specially formulated for use in Indian washing machines. The numbers looked promising, but the company noticed one glaring oddity in its data gathering: 70 percent of washing machine sales came from just one Indian state, Punjab. Something did not seem right. "We dug deeper," recounts Micky Pant, "and we were amused to discover that most washing machines were actually being sold into roadside restaurants, where Punjabi entrepreneurs modified them to produce lassi, a yogurt shake that's very popular in north India." Apparently, the tax on commercial blenders was much higher at the time, so it was more economical to use washing machines to produce shakes. Luckily for Unilever, its marketing gurus discovered this hole in the plan before launching the product!

Surprises, pleasant and unpleasant, lurk at every corner as you develop your Indian marketing plan. This chapter will equip you with the vocabulary to successfully market your products and services into India.

Twenty-first-century Indian buyers are as demanding as those in the West. It is a mistake to underestimate their expectations. "They will not hesitate to write to the CEO if they are unhappy and will expect an answer in twenty-four hours," warns Pawan Goenka, now president of automaker Mahindra & Mahindra after a successful fourteen-year career at General Motors in the United States. When India was supply-constrained, it used to be easy for Western companies to sell yesterday's technology in-country. In modern India, that is a recipe for failure.

Just as important, don't assume that your competition is going to be limited to familiar Western or Japanese companies. You may find some strong Indian competition with names like Bombay Dyeing, Godrej, Good Knight, Nirma, Parryware, or Tata, depending on your industry or product. While some practices and preferences may seem unusual to you, you maximize your chances of success if you make the effort to understand and respect the country and its values.

For most foreign companies, India is a marathon, not a sprint. "The Indian market develops in an evolutionary manner, and is seldom revolutionary. India may test your patience, but it is a successful democracy and sometimes solutions take time," cautions R. Gopalakrishnan, executive director at Tata Sons, the holding company for the Tata group, which is responsible for almost 3 percent of India's GDP.

"Be aware of the vast diversity of language, culture, and income," advises Vivek Kudva, president of California-based

Franklin Templeton's India arm, which manages more than $4 billion in assets for Indian investors. "This requires businesses to adopt a flexible strategy in order to respond to diversities across the various states."

Sales patterns for individual products vary considerably from region to region, driven by demographics, tastes, religious practices, incomes, climate, language, and many other factors. Be cautious when generalizing from localized test-marketing efforts.

Market Segments and Trends

India's 1.1 billion population consists of about 220 million households. Half of the population is under age twenty-five, and about 30 percent live in about three hundred towns and cities. The gross domestic product is growing at about 9 percent, making India the world's second fastest-growing major economy.

Growth and urbanization induce mobility. The centuries-old "joint family" structure in which adult sons continue to live with their parents well beyond getting married and having their own children has started to change all over India. However, a majority of Indian households still have three generations living under the same roof.

Socioeconomic Classes

About one in twenty Indians qualifies as middle class by American standards. While the ratio seems small, it still translates to a population of almost sixty million individuals, many of whom have not already solidified their brand preferences for products and services that middle-class Americans consider mainstream. This is a promising market opportunity in and of itself. You are probably reading this book because of your interest or your company's interest in this segment of the population.

In a May 2007 study titled "The Bird of Gold," McKinsey Global Institute forecasts that by the year 2025, 41 percent of Indians will be middle class, making a population of 581 million individuals. The study also shows that the share of total consumption by the middle class will grow from 18 percent in 2005 to 59 percent in 2025. The report is based on relatively conservative assumptions, and it is quite possible that India may achieve those numbers sooner. Even if the projections turn out to be overoptimistic, Western firms cannot afford to ignore a market developing at that kind of pace.

You may see reports from various sources that peg the Indian middle class at three hundred million individuals. In fact, President George W. Bush mentioned that number in his visit to Hyderabad in March 2006. But my research and experience leads me to believe that this number is grossly inflated. It's my view that Western firms seeking to expand their business in India should not base projections on this number; it will lead to unattainable expectations and the inevitable frustration that follows when sales targets are not met.

The upper class gets more than its fair share of media coverage in India. There are probably fewer than four million Indians who are above middle class. They travel globally for vacations, buy luxury cars, designer clothing, and top-of-the-line electronics, and may own multiple homes. According to reports from Merrill Lynch, the number of Indians with assets exceeding $1 million is growing at 20 percent per year and numbers more than one hundred thousand as of this writing. I suspect that these numbers don't include the full impact of the underground economy in India; many wealthy Indians live below the radar of such studies but will buy your company's products and services. Above the radar, *Forbes* magazine reported that in 2008, India had a total of fifty-two billionaires, compared to twenty-four in Japan and thirty in China.

Professor C. K. Prahalad of the University of Michigan Business School makes a strong business case for serving bottom-of-the-pyramid consumers—those who earn less than the equivalent of $1,500 per year in purchasing power. With examples drawn from all over the world, he shows how large multinational corporations can profit from providing innovative services and products to four billion impoverished consumers worldwide, of which at least seven hundred million live in India. Prahalad encourages large companies to create the capacity to consume among the poor by offering affordable price points, by intense distribution to stores located within a short walk of the home or place of work, and by making products available at the moment when the poor have the cash in hand to buy immediately. If you and your company are ready for breakthrough thinking, I highly recommend his 2005 book, *The Fortune at the Bottom of the Pyramid.*

Rural India

While the country is urbanizing rapidly, about two-thirds of the population still live in its 640,000 villages. Conventional wisdom dictates that new entrants to India can simply start in the top cities, where interest and demand in new products and technologies would be highest. That is not always true. ICICI Bank realized that modern technology provided the best way to provide last-mile connectivity to reach rural consumers, most of whom don't have a bank account and a significant percentage of whom might be illiterate. The bank uses biometric-smart ATM cards that authenticate rural customers based on fingerprints and can work offline in the field but can also communicate with the central information system so that paperwork is virtually eliminated. And rural customers don't have to memorize PIN numbers, either. "We might witness an interesting situation where we will retrofit what we will be doing in rural India into urban India," chuckles K. V. Kamath, managing director of ICICI Bank, the second largest in the country. Kamath incidentally was declared Asian Businessman of the Year by *Forbes* magazine in 2007.

Indian Seasons

Unique seasonal factors affect the sales cycle in India. Hindu festivals such as Diwali drive much spending in autumn, especially of consumables and some gifts. Christmas wasn't much of a factor outside Mumbai and Goa in the past, but globalization is starting to alter this.

Weddings are another major driver of both consumable and durable spending. Astrology determines three auspicious seasons when it is acceptable for most Hindus to marry, especially in north India, and much consumption is clustered around those periods. When steel billionaire Laxmi Mittal spent a reported $55 million on his daughter Vanisha's wedding in June 2004, the world took notice. But many Indian families spend a large percentage of their personal assets on the weddings of their children; some even take loans to finance the nuptials.

The summer monsoon rains can spike or depress demand in most regions between June and September. The arrival of the monsoon season is variable; it takes roughly five weeks from touching coastal Kerala in the south to reaching the northern Himalayan mountain ranges. There is also a winter monsoon season, but the rains are not as heavy and mostly affect southern India.

Market research based on income numbers will often cause gross understatement of your potential. This is partly because much of the available money comes from the underground economy and partly because Indians often understate even their legal income in surveys, anonymous or not, since they do not want to attract attention to themselves. For these reasons, consumption research is often more reliable than income research.

Middle-Class Trends: The Six Cs

The six Cs that drive change in modern middle-class urban India are credit, cars, condominium ownership, *cchutti* (vacations), cable TV, and cell phones.

Credit

Consumer credit is a relatively new phenomenon in India. While older Indians are not used to the idea of spending what they have not already earned, Indians born after about 1980 are far more open to using credit facilities. The concept of equal, or equated monthly installments (EMI), for repayment of loans is relatively new and has become pervasive among younger Indians. Financial institutions have become quite aggressive in promoting credit for the purchase of durables and homes even though extensive identity records and payment histories are not yet available.

For loans to individual borrowers, ICICI Bank uses both field investigation agencies and credit-processing agencies as part of a comprehensive due-diligence process, which includes visits to the workplaces and homes of the borrower. "In making our credit decisions, we have recently started drawing upon reports from the Credit Information Bureau India Ltd. [CIBIL]. However, CIBIL does not yet provide a credit score," explains Kamath of ICICI Bank. Ten percent of this credit bureau is owned by American credit information vendor TransUnion and another 10 percent by business information provider Dun & Bradstreet, with the balance owned by financial institutions that operate in India.

Consumer payment by debit and credit cards and by check ("cheque"* in Indian English) is on the rise, but cash still rules India. Entities that have billing relationships with consumers often depend on home visits for billing and collections. This may include the cable TV provider, the milkman, and the newspaper delivery person. Some products and services are primarily prepaid. Cellular phone service is the most visible example. A majority of Indian cell phone ("mobile phone") numbers are prepaid accounts.

Inspired by the success of Grameen Bank in neighboring Bangladesh, micro-financing is starting to affect the lower economic rungs of India, in both rural and urban areas.

Cars

For decades after independence, the Indian automobile market was flat; most middle-class families depended upon scooters and motorcycles for transportation. Those who could afford to buy a car had very limited choices, waited months to receive allocation, and generally paid cash. Today, there is a wide range of affordable choices ranging from tiny subcompacts to large SUVs. The impending launch of the Tata Nano, the word's least expensive car at under $3,000, is expected to bring cars to the pocket-

---

*In this chapter, the Indian English equivalent of an American English word will appear in parentheses; you can also find all these terms in this book's glossary. For still more Indian English terms, visit www.amritt.com/IndianEnglish.html.

books of a whole new category of Indians. Today, product is sold from stock and is home-delivered. Installment loans for cars are routine. Families with one car per adult are not uncommon in the urban upper middle class. In 2007, approximately 1.5 million cars were produced in India. In addition, another million commercial vehicles and three-wheelers as well as about eight million scooters and motorcycles were added to the roads. Note that scooters and motorcycles are used as primary transportation in India, rather than for weekend recreation.

Many social, economic, and business changes are resulting from automobile ownership in today's India—but not in quite the same way that they happened in the United States. For example, gas stations ("petrol pumps") now feature convenience stores, drive-through or drive-up eateries are becoming more common, the affluent are buying weekend country houses ("farms"), and housewives are becoming more mobile. However, many Indians who can afford cars can also afford a full-time chauffeur ("driver") and equip him with a mobile phone. Car care is relegated to hired help, and most Indians treat their automobile as a utility item, not one to be loved and treasured. A minor ding or scratch does not bother the average Indian as much as it does an American, for example. Families often don't treat cars as personal possessions of the individuals; car keys may hang at a common location in the living room rather than on one person's keychain. In a multicar family, the grandfather may use the son's or daughter-in-law's car or vice versa without much thought, and spouses might exchange cars for convenience as needed. The American habit of leaving numerous personal objects in the automobile is not as common in India.

Condominium Ownership

In the past, many middle-class Indians worked and saved for most of their careers so that they could afford to buy a single-family house sometime shortly before retirement. With modern residential towers that offer apartment condominiums ("flats") for fifty or more families where a single bungalow may once have stood, large numbers of young urban couples are buying homes on credit and feeding a construction boom across urban India. Many cities are growing outward rapidly, with entire new townships of high-rise and midrise construction appearing. The associations that manage and run these condominiums are referred to as societies in much of India. When a Mumbai resident mentions that people in his society don't like loud parties, for example, he is referring to his neighbors and not to society at large.

The construction boom has fueled new demand for home appliances, furniture, bathroom fixtures, and all the accoutrements of high-rise living. Any company in a related business can potentially flourish in India.

Cchutti *(Vacations)*

In the last generation, almost all vacation time was reserved for visiting relatives or going on pilgrimages to religious sites. The idea of taking a weeklong vacation during which you stay in hotels and don't meet extended family is relatively new. Still, more and more Indians today are visiting domestic tourist spots, taking weekend trips to Southeast Asia, and enjoying longer vacations to Europe, Australia, and North America. The availability of and tendency to use credit to finance a vacation is a novel phenomenon with increasing appeal. Some young adults might even choose to defer buying furniture or large appliances and use their credit to pay for a trip.

*   *   *

While the previous four trends are limited to middle- and upper-class Indians, the next two, cable TV and cell phones, are starting to transform the lower socioeconomic strata of society, even as their impact on middle-class India starts to be understood by marketers.

Cable TV

The average middle-class household now receives cable TV from a very local provider but has a wide choice of international, national, and local-language channels available. While much of the media consumed is produced domestically, there is considerable awareness—through news, programming, and movies—about global trends and consumption patterns. Cable TV is now accessible to virtually all urban middle-class Indians. There is some direct-to-home broadcasting available, but for marketing purposes it is similar to cable.

Access to more than three hundred channels of programming is changing society in ways that are still being researched and understood. For example, Professor Emily Oster of the University of Chicago studied cable TV's impact on gender attitudes in rural India and found convincing evidence that the expanded worldview is equivalent to about three to five years of education and produces significant improvements in women's status relating to school enrollment, decrease in preference for male babies, and better spacing between pregnancies.

Cell Phones

By the time they acquired their first cell phone, most Americans already had a land-based phone line, a computer, and perhaps even an Internet connection. Not so in India.

Unlike the United States, handsets are not subsidized by cellular carriers in India. Yet, driven by the lowest calling rates in the world and helped by the fact that incoming calls are free, more than 165 million Indians now own cell phones. That number is rising so rapidly, it's likely to be substantially higher by the time you read this. Indians are vigorous users of text messaging ("SMS") as well. Micro-entrepreneurs such as pushcart vendors who sell vegetables from door to door, plumbers, water filter sales and service people, and a multitude of other mobile professions have been transformed and increased their productivity and earning power as a result of cell phones.

At about the time of this writing, one major provider

began offering unsubsidized handsets for 777 rupees (under $20); another responded by offering its handset for 666 rupees (less than $17). Almost every new subscriber is someone who has never had a home telephone ("landline") before and likely does not have access to a personal computer at home. More new phones are being installed in India than in China today. Most growth will occur in the rural areas. And the behavior and consumption patterns of these newly connected masses are being altered by technology in unique ways. For example, C.K. Prahalad writes about how small-boat fishermen in southern India now call ahead to check the price of their product in two nearby ports to determine where to dock and sell their catch of the day.

SELLING TO THE INDIAN GOVERNMENT AND TO INDIAN BUSINESSES

Many of the factors relating to Indian consumers also apply when your product is meant for business, industry, or government. Your company's sales to Indian businesses and governments (at the state and federal level) could grow at 30 percent per year—or they could be flat, depending on how effectively you address Indian needs.

Let's talk about a few of the surprises in this country.

Some business-to-business advertisements show up in consumer media such as newspapers, billboards, even the occasional television commercial. You may see industrial pumps advertised in the news section of the daily paper, or billboards for steel billets and the like. Most are genuine ads run by smart companies and agencies that have figured the most cost-effective way to reach their specific audience. In the competitive job market that is India today, you may also see shopping-mall ads from major IT and industrial companies that are appealing to potential employees, not to customers.

Indian companies tend to be very capital-efficient, and many are extremely aggressive about cash-flow management. So they look for products that don't waste resources and payment plans that enable maximum liquidity. Companies will gladly pay a premium for a feature or benefit that they especially value or one that gives them a real competitive edge.

The Indian unit of Cummins is the market leader in the power rental business. Rather than selling diesel generator sets, Cummins Power Generation rents the units for periods ranging from a few weeks to a few years to customers such as rice mills, bottling plants, stone quarries, utilities, large hotels and commercial complexes, and even mini cement plants.

As Western companies enter the Indian market, it is important to understand that—as is the case in any country—incumbent players have the advantage. India is one of the few markets where European, Russian, Asian, and American vendors will compete head-to-head in the defense, aerospace, and nuclear technology industries. Nimble and responsive companies will win the big deals. Unlike other emerging economies, India's free press and democracy work in favor of creating transparency in government purchases.

Further, if you happen to compete against Indian public-sector companies for government work, the public-sector vendors are given some price preference. Government entities tend to favor the lowest bidder. If a vendor meets the minimum specifications and is the low bidder, it can win the job. According to Scott Bayman, who recently retired from General Electric, "You could be the second lowest bidder, you may have a much superior product, but if the lower price still meets the spec then it is difficult to sell up at that point. Companies that have superior products and services must sell the advantages so that they get put into the specifications and requirements." Bayman adds that it's important for you to realize in going to developing countries that you are not going to change the world. You must adapt your company's strategy, objectives, culture, and processes to the local environment. That doesn't mean you have to sell out; by all means, take the best practices from your company. You do have to adapt those to work in the environment in which you're doing business, though. There is going to be corruption; it is a way of life. You can fight it, you *need* to do that, you *need* to protest when you lose an order for the wrong reasons. You can go to court as GE has done but you are not going to make these issues go away immediately. You will not create change overnight.

There are no shortcuts to success when selling to governments. The Indian government is made up of people; you have to be introduced, establish relationships, have patience, and know when to follow up. Heed the advice of John Triplett, an American who has lived in India for seven years and was head of consulting firm Parsons Brinckerhoff's India operation: "Be prepared to accept that most things move slowly in India. Something may be promised for next week, so don't be discouraged or give up should it not happen. Follow up the matter, and see if there is anything that you can do to help the progress."

Marketing: The Four Ps

Let's look at the four Ps of marketing—product, place, price, and promotion—and how they play out in India.

Products and Brands

Product designs and service offerings must be modified to Indian needs or else they may fail to attract a market. For example, comfortable, spacious rear seats are crucial in a society where many cars are chauffeur-driven. So successful carmakers have adjusted their designs to improve comfort, space, and door access in rear compartments. On the other hand, frost-free refrigerators are not such a big deal when you have servants who can clean the fridge and you lose power three times a day anyway.

Blenders ("mixies") for the Indian housewife had better survive grinding lentils and nuts on a routine basis. Washing machines need to handle the six-yard-long sarees worn by many Indian women. Any product that uses electricity needs to deal with extreme fluctuations in voltage and frequency as well as situations where the power is unavailable for hours at a time. Johnson & Johnson found that it had to reformulate its adhesive bandages to accommodate not only the higher heat and humidity of India, but also the somewhat oilier Indian skin.

Eateries, grocery stores, and anyone handling food products must be sensitive to the needs of vegetarians as well as of Hindus, who don't eat beef, and Muslims, who don't eat pork. While there are many vegetarians in India, a lot of Indians will eat "nonveg" once or twice a week. Along the coastal area, much of the population eats fish. Indian law requires packaged foods to be clearly labeled as vegetarian or not.

When I bought a Sony video camera on a recent trip to India, the store sent a senior employee to my mother's home to teach us how to use it. The next day, a Sony employee called to set up a further appointment for in-home training. This is not unusual. If you sell water purifiers, microwave ovens, televisions, computers, or printers, count on offering in-home training, service, and repair.

In India, services are often differentiated by class. Movie theaters ("cinema halls") have always offered premium-priced tickets for seats toward the rear. New multiplexes have come up in major cities that sell tickets at substantially higher prices than regular theaters and have created a genre of niche-market Indian movies that did not exist before. Service on trains is layered into First AC (air-conditioned), Second AC, Third AC, Chair Car, Non-AC, and finally nonreserved benches. Restaurants offer the same menu at different price levels, depending on whether you sit in the open or air-conditioned area of the same facility. Some customers will pay premium prices simply to distinguish themselves as higher in class.

Prior to liberalization, anything "imported" was considered superior, and you may still see some brands emphasizing their foreign origin. Indian brands historically tried to match that by imprinting EXPORT QUALITY on their products. But this attitude seems to be fading away as many overseas brands become mainstream and Indians begin to feel proud of domestic brands such as Tata, Mahindra, Dabur, Amul, Haldiram, and MTR.

Western brand associations don't always translate in India. Hyundai is considered a premium name in India; Samsung was recognized in-country long before it became respectable in the United States. Suzuki is associated more with cars than motorcycles. Indians are quite brand-conscious and relatively conservative about trying new brands. For example, Lexus is not recognized much in India, but Mercedes is deeply rooted as a top car brand. Tupperware found it worthwhile to promote some of its products by partnering with locally popular brands; Dalda shortening and cooking oil were sold in reusable Tupperware jars as a way to promote Tupperware.

TROPICANA OVERCOMES TASTE AND PRICE BARRIERS

When PepsiCo's Tropicana entered the fruit juice market in India in 1998, the sales of pure packaged juice were less than $10 million per year. Home-grown Dabur Foods had a head start of three years with its Real brand. According to Tropicana's advertising agency, Ulka (an affiliate of Foote, Cone & Belding), consumer studies in India were also discouraging. Indian consumers preferred a sweeter taste; they also associated the yellow color of the orange juice with mangoes, and its aroma with preservatives, contradicting Tropicana's image of "natural." In addition, the product was to be priced 40 percent higher than Real and other competitors.

Indians don't like drinking cold, sour liquids early in the morning, so selling the juice as a breakfast drink was not going to work. It was better to propose the drink as a filler between meals. Indians had historically preferred freshly squeezed juices whether made at home or purchased from a roadside vendor. However, people were starting to become concerned about hygiene among roadside vendors, and Indian women were growing more responsive to the convenience factor of packaged products as opposed to the mess of squeezing the juice at home. Exercising and eating right were becoming more important to Indians, too, and this was starting to manifest itself with decreased use of oils and fats in cooking.

One of Tropicana's insights about healthy foods was that a compromise on taste was acceptable if the food was perceived to be healthy. Therefore, the firm's entire marketing strategy revolved around turning its taste disadvantage into an advantage. A brand perceived as healthier could also command a better price.

The advertising campaign used the slogan "The Taste of Good Health" to overcome the negative reaction to taste. Television commercials featured gymnasts, ballerinas, and basketball players to reinforce not only the feeling of health and fitness but also high class as depicted in international imagery, to justify the higher price. By the year 2000, Tropicana's vigorous and consistent campaign enabled it to edge out Real in both market leadership and mindshare. The Tropicana campaign won an Effie Award in 2002 for advertising effectiveness. By 2004, Tropicana management was reporting India to be one of the top ten markets for the brand worldwide—and growing at double-digit rates.

Place: Channels and Competition

In 1963, the first computer at any educational institution in India was installed at the Indian Institute of Technology Kanpur. It was an IBM 1620 all the way from the United States. It arrived at its final destination on a bullock cart! In twenty-first-century India, bullock carts are still used for physical distribution of many items.

Distribution of consumer goods in India tends to be regionally and locally fragmented. You may need to appoint several distributors for the country. Warehouses ("godowns") may be owned and operated separately from the small business that physically delivers goods to the final point of sale. Agents, importers, sub-importers, brokers, forwarders, "stockists," and other middlemen may affect your particular supply chain. Many of these middlemen operate on low margins and minimal service: This can be a problem if your product requires a high level of attention along the supply chain. India's low-tech supply chains can also be subject to pilferage and product degradation.

Transportation logistics from the point of import or manufacture to the final retailer may be more complex. Trains, trucks, vans, three-wheelers, and even bicycle-rickshaws, animal carts, and hand-pushed street trolleys may be deployed before your product reaches the customer. If your packaging is not designed to deal with the intervening heat, dust, thunderstorms, humidity, and other abuse, your customers' out-of-box experience may suffer substantially.

Modern enclosed, air-conditioned shopping malls are a relatively new notion in India. Ansal Plaza in New Delhi, the Crossroads Mall in Mumbai, and Spencer Plaza in Chennai were the leaders in 2000. Since then, urban India has witnessed an explosion of shopping centers funded mostly by large professional real estate developers such as DLF in the Delhi area. Given the relatively high price of land, many malls tend to be more vertical than horizontal, with layers of tightly packed underground parking and three to eight floors of shopping. Many young Indian professionals are attracted to the modern layout, and some malls play loud rock music in the public areas. On busy weekends, malls may be forced to limit customer entry due to over-crowding.

Multibrand retailing is still off limits to foreign compa-nies, so you won't see Wal-Mart or Tesco stores in India. More than 90 percent of retail stores ("shops") in India are single-location and family-owned. Many are tiny, to the point that customers actually stand outside the store and ask the owner to pick out the products they need for the day. Even the larger ones offer limited visibility of your product and packaging. Product decisions are made by the customer prior to approaching the store or driven by advice from the salesperson or cashier. In many middle-class neighborhoods, the retailer delivers goods to the customer's home based on a phone or in-person order. Durable products may be displayed in showrooms, but these spaces are often small by American standards.

For years, the term *supermarket* was associated with nonprofit cooperative organizations, with the notable exception of Nilgiri's in Bangalore. Since the late 1990s, several new chains have sprung up: Subhiksha, FoodWorld run by the RP Goenka group, Food Bazaar from clothing re-tailer Pantaloons, and most recently Reliance Fresh. Many supermarket companies also own store chains in other formats for electronics, clothing, appliances, and so forth. For example, Pantaloons operates Big Bazaar, a discount store, and Reliance has launched Reliance Mart, a super-store with more than eighty thousand products. Wal-Mart is entering India with a joint-venture partner to run whole-sale cash-and-carry centers serving retail store owners.

After initial hiccups, several American fast-food chains have established successful franchises in India. McDonald's entered with two separate joint-venture partners, one centered in Delhi and another in Mumbai. Many McDonald's locations provide delivery to home or office. Pizza Hut has 135 stores in thirty-four cities in India and plans to increase that number to 200. Subway Sandwich, Domino's Pizza, even T.G.I. Friday's and Ruby Tuesday have operations in India.

The leader in high-priced athletic footwear in India is Reebok by a long shot, followed by its affiliate, Adidas. In the mid-1990s, when Reebok entered the Indian market, no one believed that Indians would pay 2,500 rupees for a pair of shoes. But, says Micky Pant, who was recruited from Pepsi India to lead Reebok's entry, "We came in with professional world-class stores, high-quality product, and excellent point-of-sale fixtures. Customers began spending money on us, and soon we were running at very healthy margins."

Direct selling and network marketing had existed in India for decades, but American companies only entered this arena in the 1990s. Today, companies in this sector—including Amway, Avon, Herbalife, and Tupperware—operate with varying degrees of success in India. In most of the rest of the world, an Amway customer orders the product over the phone or the Internet. However, the company found that in India, most customers need to touch and feel a new product before ordering it, so they built more than forty-eight pickup centers.

In India, competition can emerge from unexpected sources. Unilever had a very strong brand with its Surf detergent in India. Micky Pant recalls meeting "a simple Gujarati fellow named Karsanbhai Patel" and not being impressed. Patel produced a detergent called Nirma that sold for a fraction of the cost of Surf. But when reports began trickling in of its rising sales, Pant recalls, "I sent one of our trainees to count the number of trucks leaving the Nirma factory to estimate his production, and we could not believe the numbers. He was producing over a hundred thousand tons of Nirma at a time when Surf was selling a quarter of that figure!" More recently, in 2002, incumbent cell phone operators were given a run for their money when Reliance Communications sprang onto the scene and rose to the top within eight months of its launch.

Sometimes an unlikely partner can be worth the investment time and effort. Western Union approached the government-owned India Post for help on its money transfer service. Note that India Post has always offered domestic money orders, in which the mailman ("postman") delivers cash to people's homes; the post office also offers very basic banking services in the form of a passbook savings account. After an eighteen-month discussion and negotiation, India Post rolled out its Western Union money transfer service. Today, eighty-five hundred of Western Union's forty thousand India locations are housed inside post offices across the nation, mostly in rural and semi-urban areas. Over a six-year period, Western Union India managing director Anil Kapur and his team have trained more than ten thousand postal employees in using the money transfer system. Remittances to India have grown at 90 percent per year for the last several years. "Postmasters like our services because we drive new business into their offices, especially in the form of Postal Savings Accounts. The postmaster in a rural area is hugely influential in the community—he or she gets to advise who goes to which college, often makes wedding matches, and is generally trusted by the villagers," adds Kapur.

Price

On most consumer packaged goods ("fast-moving consumer goods" or FMCG), regulations require that the manufacturer state a maximum retail price, including all taxes. Retailers cannot sell the product for more than that price (called the MRP), regardless of any further convenience that might be offered, such as being open at night or located inside a hotel lobby.

Since labor is inexpensive and storage space is at a premium, Indian consumers are not attracted to the kinds of oversize packages that Americans love to buy at Costco and Sam's Club. In fact, Indians will pay a slight price premium for something that is packaged and sold in single-serving portions. In an interview with Rediff.com, Amway India CEO William Pinckney related an important lesson: "A one-size-fits-all strategy won't be successful in India. We have a portfolio of 450 products that are all available in one size each. Except in India, that is. Indians don't like economy-size packs until they've tried the product earlier.

Accordingly, we launched our cleaning and personal care products in various sizes—big, medium, small, and even single-use sachets."

Single-use packaging is offered in India for ongoing consumption, not just for trial or travel purposes. Occasional users of a product won't buy it in any other form—and they can make up a very substantial market, be it for diapers, cookies, cigarettes, or shampoos. Bulky or complex packaging also draws frowns in India unless it serves a secondary purpose, such as a storage jar for other products. In some cases, pay-as-you-go or pay-per-use pricing is a better way to attract and retain Indian consumers.

If your product or service from Western markets appears to be a premium-priced offering in India, consultants will often advise you to simply skim the market and deal only with the premium segment. That could be a good first step, but it is often worthwhile to work in parallel to design or formulate a mass-market product. It may take a few months or years to launch the product, but it gives you the opportunity to sell a lot more units over time and increase your overall profits from India.

Indians tend to use durable goods such as house furniture for longer periods of time than do Western societies. Inexpensive and readily available repair services are a significant reason for this, as is the tendency to be functional and frugal. So a significant price premium for product reliability may not attract a mainstream audience.

Promotion and Advertising

On a recent trip to Hyderabad, I was watching television in the café over breakfast at a hotel and saw a famous face pitching an unusual product.

The product was Binani Cement. The celebrity in the forty-second television commercial was one of India's most storied entertainment celebrities: Amitabh Bachchan, known to Indians as the Big B. The theme of the advertisement compares Binani to the Big B. Can you imagine Michael Douglas or Tom Cruise promoting concrete on mainstream television? Welcome to twenty-first-century India!

Upon researching the subject, I found that in the previous year, Binani had aired more than a thousand television spots on thirty broadcast and cable channels, ranging from CNBC India to vernacular sitcoms; they also put up over five hundred billboards and bought print advertising in mainstream and business publications featuring the celebrity endorsement.

Celebrity sponsors are often referred to as brand ambassadors in India, although sometimes all they do is offer their likeness to billboards or print ads. Cricket and Bollywood are the biggest providers of such celebrities. Veteran movie star Amitabh Bachchan sells everything from Pepsi to ICICI Bank, Parker pens, Nerolac paints, Reid & Taylor suits, and Maruti's Versa van, in addition to Binani Cement.

Cricket phenomenon Sachin Tendulkar has endorsed Adidas, Pepsi, Canon, TVS Motorcycles, ESPN Star Sports, and then some. Only a few foreign faces have broad appeal in India. Micky Pant remembers how, in the 1980s, his company could sponsor the Sri Lankan cricket team for the cost of providing sports kits to them. Today, sponsorships with top celebrities run in the millions of dollars.

Global brands used to run their Western ads and slogans in India. Pepsi changed that with *Yeh Dil Maange More,* a mixture of Hindi and English that translates to "This [my] heart asks for more." The television campaign was a phenomenal success; the slogan transcended advertising to reach into common parlance, even becoming the title of a Bollywood movie. Indian media is now rife with slogans that speak the vernacular mixture of Hindi, English, and other languages that best represent popular culture in-country.

Today, India is one of the few significant markets where all major media—magazines, newspapers, billboards, television, radio, and Internet—are either growing or relatively stable. The wall between editorial and advertising is not terribly rigid at some publications. Sophisticated consumers generally know which media can be trusted more for editorial coverage.

About sixteen million new television sets are sold each year in India today. Thanks to affordable repair labor rates and the tendency not to discard working products, most sets have an operating life of more than ten years. Television reaches over a hundred million Indian households with free over-the-air services offered via state-owned Doordarshan, which does carry commercials. More than half of these households also subscribe to cable TV, which provides dozens of additional local and global channels. The National Readership Studies Council estimates that about 230 million Indians watch satellite television in an average week based on its 2006 study.

Radio covers more than 90 percent of the population, with state-owned All India Radio operating several hundred AM ("medium wave") stations. Privately owned and operated FM stations are growing rapidly and are often a great medium to reach young consumers.

Most major Indian cities support multiple English-language newspapers; many papers are printed in multiple cities simultaneously. The *Times of India* enjoys the largest circulation among English-language dailies with more than seven million readers, but it is the only English paper among the top ten dailies, according to the Indian Readership Survey of 2006. In any given city, a local vernacular newspaper might be the leading seller. *Dainik Jagran* (daily awakening), printed in twenty-eight local editions, is the largest circulating Hindi newspaper and dominates central and northern India with about nineteen million readers. Newspaper circulation will continue to grow due to increasing literacy, increasing wealth, and increasing population.

Among magazines, the leader is *Saras Salil*—a Hindi magazine with seven million readers. The leading English magazine is the weekly *India Today,* with about half that circulation.

You cannot look at subscription numbers to measure the reach of the Internet. That's because many Indians access the Web primarily at work; also, about one-third of all users use only cybercafés for access. It is not unusual for a small business person to spend thirty minutes a day at the cybercafé in his or her neighborhood.

Advertising agencies are quite sophisticated about understanding local preferences for deploying regional campaigns within India. Most major global agencies have affiliates in India, and there are a number of excellent home-grown shops as well. If you sell to Indian consumers, you may need to advertise in local languages. For example, Western Union runs no national advertising in India, and most of its spending is in regional languages. India was the first country where the company even translated its distinctive logo into local language signage.

Another example of developing local sensibilities is Whirlpool. The company was a late entrant in the Indian market and had to battle well-established local brands. In addition, most Indians affluent enough to own a washing machine already had household help to do the laundry. Indian women felt that it was easier to control a maid than a machine and that hand washing was the best way to remove collar and cuff stains. So agency FCB Ulka highlighted the agitator mechanism in the Whirlpool machines, comparing it favorably with the effectiveness of hand washing. The campaign was a grand success. If you are not in the washing machine business, the takeaway is to understand Indian attitudes and leverage them right rather than fight to change them.

On the other hand, some subjects that may be sensitive in the West are noncontroversial in Indian advertising. Ads for condoms appear on billboards and television. A public awareness campaign, *Condom Bindaas Bol* (utter the word *condom* without reservation or embarrassment) won a United Nations award in 2007.

Amul Butter has an irreverent and humorous billboard ("hoarding") campaign that refers to current events. In a recent month in Mumbai, Amul declared, *Bole to, Apun Saath hai Baba*—Mumbai street language for "Say there, brother, we are on your side"—and featured Bollywood superstar Sanjay Dutt (popularly known as Sanju Baba), who had just entered jail for possessing prohibited weapons. A couple of weeks earlier, the butter company poked fun at India's Communist Parties for raising a furor over the US–India nuclear deal with the quip "Seeing red? Try yellow!" The background showed President Bush and Prime Minister Singh shaking hands and eating creamy yellow buttered sandwiches.

Marketing to Youth in India

One of my most insightful friends has spent a career marketing American brands in India. He explains that Indian youth have a Western crust but an Indian core. They will borrow from the West but not ape it. While they have an increased propensity to spend compared with the previous generation, they still have tremendous respect for their parents and will defer to their elders in major decisions. But unlike their elders, they have a very high degree of self-confidence, and their role model choices are driven by success.

If you watch MTV on cable television in India, you will quickly see how a successful American youth brand has taken its essence but applied it to new content, which the Viacom International's India unit network creates in India for India. You will see Indian VJs presenting Indian shows, but the styles and attitude are unmistakably MTV.

In *Businessworld* magazine, the managing director of Levi Strauss's Indian unit, Shumone Chatterjee, was quoted as saying that sales had tripled in Bangalore in three years. Levi's has found it profitable not only to sell its premium 501 and Red Loop jeans in India but also to create a low-end nondenim brand, Levi's Sykes, which sells for a third the price of 501s. Levi Strauss has more than ninety stores in India, including a nine-thousand-square-foot unit in downtown Bangalore, its largest in Asia.

Conclusion

While the principles of marketing remain the same, when you approach India its practice may differ considerably from your expectations. If you don't listen very carefully to the differences and then act to leverage them to your advantage, chances are high that you will compromise your success. Winning in India's market sometimes requires abandoning cherished beliefs about what works; sometimes, too, it requires adapting not only your distribution and advertising but your product and pricing as well. For Western brands that are willing to invest the time, effort, and management bandwidth, India offers plenty of promise. Fortunately for you, many of your competitors will approach the Indian market without serious interest in making these investments. So when you read about someone failing in India, it is just an opportunity for someone else to succeed.

CHAPTER 6

Finance

In this chapter, we will review banking, venture capital, private equity, and the public markets in India. We will also look at flows of money into India from these sources, as well as from remittances. Finally, we briefly discuss joint ventures and cross-border mergers and acquisitions.

Banking and Money

India's central bank is the Reserve Bank of India, headquartered in south Mumbai. While it controls monetary policy (including price stability and availability of credit) as well as printing and circulation of currency, it is a direct instrument of the federal government, and its governor has no power independent of the executive branch—unlike the American Federal Reserve. The Reserve Bank has the added responsibility of managing foreign exchange and approving foreign investment into India. Prior to liberalization, the country was short on foreign exchange, and the bank played a crucial role in allocating scarce dollars to best use. But as the economy has improved, India's exchange reserves have risen to almost embarrassing levels: $232 billion as of September 2007.

Cash and currency are far more important in the Indian economy than in developed countries. It is not unusual for large consumer purchases to involve cash payment. Paper currency (called notes, not bills, in India) comes in different sizes and colors depending on the denomination. You are most likely to encounter 20-, 50-, 100-, and 500-rupee bills. The 1,000-rupee bill, one of the physically largest currency notes in circulation anywhere in the world, is becoming more common. The bank is trying to encourage the use of coins for denominations of less than 10 rupees.

India has several state-owned and private retail banks. The State Bank of India is the largest, with 13,500 branches and five thousand ATMs in-country as well as some operations in thirty-five other countries. While it is traded on the Bombay Stock Exchange, most of the bank's stock is still held by the government. More highly valued by the stock market is ICICI Bank, with just 950 branches and thirty-three hundred ATMs in India and a presence in seventeen countries.

New York–based Citibank opened its first Indian office in what is now Kolkata in 1902. It began offering retail banking in India in 1985, according to Sanjay Nayar, the bank's CEO for South Asia. With thirty-nine branches in twenty-seven cities, India's largest foreign bank now has more than seven million retail customers. "Citi India is one of the fastest-growing businesses within the Citi world," claims a proud Nayar, who started with the bank in 1985 and has a degree in mechanical engineering.

Other foreign banks with significant Indian operations include the ABN AMRO Bank, American Express Bank, Bank of America, Deutsche Bank, HSBC, and Standard Chartered Bank.

Venture Capital and Private Equity

If I closed my eyes and just listened to the din, I might have thought I was in a singles bar. The excited voices, the throbbing tension—I could almost smell the breathless anticipation. Only the music was missing.

Yet it was daytime at Mumbai's gleaming Hyatt Regency conference center in December 2006.

In an elbow-to-elbow throng at the national summit of The Indus Entrepreneur (TiE), it seemed that I greeted a new venture capitalist every ten minutes. Since I often help American companies buy from offshore vendors, the organizers had thought it might be helpful if I spoke to start-up entrepreneurs on how to market their products globally. While I enjoyed speaking to the young would-be entrepreneurs, it was just as much fun to watch early-stage investors interact with the start-ups. A few weeks earlier, I had witnessed a similar occurrence at a conference in New Delhi's Maurya hotel.

Almost every California blue-chip venture capital (VC) partnership now has an Indian operation. During the dot-com boom, I had helped raise capital while on the executive team of two different start-ups; the best VCs at the time disdained investing in companies whose headquarters were farther than two hours from their own. Smart money is all about good relationships, and you can't build good relationships long-distance, I was told by VCs based on Silicon Valley's famous Sand Hill Road. "Los Angeles is too far. I don't want to *fly* to my board meetings."

Not anymore! Today, firms from the Silicon Valley such as Battery, Bessemer, BlueRun, Clearstone, Draper Fisher Jurvetson, Intel Capital, Kleiner Perkins, Mayfield, New Enterprise Associates, Norwest, Sequoia, and Walden are active in India. According to the Web site for the Indian Venture Capital Association, the total number of private-equity and venture capital deals more than doubled from 146 in 2005 to 299 in 2006. Deal value more than tripled, from $2.2 billion to $7.5 billion—and the first half of 2007 had already seen $5.6 billion in deals.

The first wave of these investors came to India looking for low-cost development centers. But very soon they began investing in companies that draw revenues from the India market. Kleiner Perkins, the fabled venture capital firm that invested in Amazon, Google, and Intuit, is bullish on its start-ups that draw revenue from India, that is, companies that sell into India rather than coming to India for low-cost labor while selling their product into the West. India has a very strong capital market that has been in place for a hundred years. "If you look at the number of billion-dollar-plus market capital companies on Indian markets, it far exceeds those in China," asserts Ajit Nazre, who

is based in California and travels to meet his Indian invest-
ees several times a year. One portfolio company, Naukri
.com, has already gone public; Cleartrip, a travel start-up,
overtook its local competitors very rapidly. Nazre funded
Cleartrip in the classic Kleiner method, when the company had little more than a team of founders and a business plan.

By 2007, another legendary VC, Sequoia Capital, had
more than thirty-five investments in India, including $20
million invested in the parent of the Café Coffee Day chain
and $30 million in the *Times of India* Web sites. It also has
investments in public companies such as the Royal Orchid
Hotels and Idea Cellular.

In the world of private equity, major players including Actis, Blackstone, Carlyle, General Atlantic, Lehman
Brothers, Oak Hill, and Warburg Pincus are active in India.
By 2001, Warburg owned 18 percent of leading cellular carrier Bharti Televentures, now known as Bharti Airtel. *BusinessWeek* magazine reported that Warburg made a $1.1
billion profit in 2005 by selling off two-thirds of its $300
million initial investment into the carrier. Indian media
noted that sale with pride, particularly because more than
half of it was executed in the single largest transaction
on the Bombay Stock Exchange, a $560 million trade ex-
ecuted flawlessly in less than thirty minutes.

General Electric sold 60 percent of its business process
outsourcing unit in India to Oak Hill and General Atlantic Partners for about $500 million in 2004. And in 2006,
Kohlberg Kravis Roberts made its first investment in India

by paying $900 million for the software business of Flex-tronics, which had about sixty-one hundred employees at the time. In 2007, Blackstone paid $200 million to acquire control of Intelenet Global Services, a growing business process outsourcing provider with over seventeen thousand employees at the time.

In 2006, Bain & Company's private-equity practice studied more than 150 deals spanning the previous five years and made a "conservative" projection that the market would triple by 2010, to almost $7 billion. But hiding behind these numbers is a more fundamental sociological factor. Historically, Indian business people resisted a sale of their company or even a significant change of operating control as a sign of failure. "His firm was sold" was almost a slur, implying near bankruptcy or liquidation. In the new India, this attitude is beginning to change, not only among the upstarts but also amid the traditional family-controlled businesses that make up the bulk of India's private sector.

India's Capital Markets

While there are twenty-two stock exchanges that list more than ten thousand companies in India, most Western corporations need to look only at two primary bourses: the Bombay Stock Exchange, established in 1875; and the National Stock Exchange, founded in 1992, in the wake of liberalization.

Located on Dalal (the word means "broker") Street in

downtown Mumbai, the Bombay Stock Exchange is the oldest operating securities market in all of Asia. The term *Dalal Street* is used as shorthand to refer to the financial markets in India. In the newer Bandra-Kurla Complex several miles north of Dalal Street is the National Stock Exchange, which is owned by several major Indian banks and financial institutions. The NSE embraced technology and new products early, and with the support of its owners quickly eclipsed the Bombay Stock Exchange in size. The stock exchanges follow a robust online trading system for both primary market offerings and secondary trading.

The markets are regulated by the Securities and Exchange Board of India (SEBI), which was established in 1992. India's markets have grown more transparent, more vibrant, and more liquid under its watch. In 2007, India's largest real estate developer, DLF Ltd., set a record with a $2.4 billion initial public offering. In 2004, Tata Consultancy Services raised $1.1 billion; the Oil and Natural Gas Corporation (ONGC), $2.2 billion. Indian investors, large and small, have the capital to fund these domestic offerings. The firms and their bankers don't need to turn to American or European markets for stock offerings. Most good public offerings have been oversubscribed several times over thanks to a combination of motivated retail and institutional investors.

By 2001, ten Indian companies had listed on the New York Stock Exchange and NASDAQ, including banks, telecommunications providers, and software services vendors. NASDAQ announced that it opened its first Asian office in Bangalore in 2001. But partly because of the 2002 passage of the US Sarbanes-Oxley Act, which is seen as onerous, and partly because of the vibrant domestic markets, American exchanges have lost their luster in India. Since then only three new companies—carmaker Tata Motors in 2004, outsourcer Patni Computer Systems in 2005, and call center operator WNS Holdings in 2006—have chosen to list in the United States, on the New York Stock Exchange. In recent years, most companies in India have found it relatively easy to raise equity capital in Mumbai.

Forbes magazine publishes an annual list of "Fabulous Fifty" large public companies in Asia. In 2007, twelve of those companies were Indian, more than from any other country.

Out of those twelve, only five had chosen to list on American exchanges. Seven of the strongest companies in India, by *Forbes*'s reckoning—ranging from power equipment maker BHEL to cement producer Grasim, engineering firm Larsen & Toubro, India's largest private-sector company Reliance Industries Ltd., and the world's lowest-cost steelmaker Tata Steel—have chosen to list only on the Indian markets.

On the other hand, companies with foreign ownership have continued to raise equity on the Indian markets. In fact, the second largest initial public offering of shares on the Indian stock market was the affiliate of London-listed Cairn Energy in January 2007. Cairn India, an oil exploration and production company, raised $1.4 billion from Indian and overseas investors. Earlier, Gillette's India operation and i-flex Solutions, a Citigroup subsidiary, also raised equity capital in India.

While the stock market is quite liquid and vibrant in India, the bond market might be characterized as less mature, even today. "Though the India equity capital markets are now well developed, debt markets lag quite a bit," admits Citigroup's Sanjay Nayar. You may find it productive to explore both local and global markets for debt funding. Corporate debt is generally a private-placement market. Large banks, mutual funds, and similar players are the principal providers of debt funding. This may change in the near future: Regulators are keen to develop a vibrant market for bonds and other private debt, and the investing public continues to have an appetite for new instruments.

Project Financing

The government of India has a strong credit record with development institutions. The country is a founding member of the Asian Development Bank, which made one hundred loans to it totaling $16.4 billion between 1986 and 2006. Current ADB loans to India are focused in road transport and energy.

In July 2007, the World Bank announced that it had increased its loans to India by 170 percent to a record $3.8 billion in a single year. India remains the largest single borrower from the bank, which employs 140 staff members on the ground in New Delhi. As of this writing, the bank has sixty-seven active projects in India with a total of $14.3 billion in outlays. It ranks India's institutions among the top 20 percent in developing countries.

Foreign Direct Investment

India attracted $6.6 billion of inward foreign direct investment (FDI) in 2005, according to the United Nations Conference on Trade and Development, and this accounted for just 3.5 percent of its gross fixed capital formation. This number is dwarfed by the $72.4 billion inflow into China, which accounted for 9.2 percent of capital formation there.

In my view, however, the difference is less stark than these numbers imply. For one thing, China's statistics appear to count flows from Hong Kong and Macau as foreign capital; too, as we saw earlier, India has a vibrant and transparent domestic capital market. Also, some experts believe that India's statistics are understated because they do not include reinvested earnings by foreign companies, venture capital investment, proceeds from foreign equity listings, foreign loans to domestic subsidiaries, and more. Even with all those adjustments, foreign investment into India still lags.

Due to a favorable tax treaty on capital gains, many investors from across the world have preferred to route their investments into India via the tiny island nation of Mauritius. This means that numbers from other countries appear distorted. Before you commit to the Mauritius route, check with your legal and investment advisers. Cyprus, Dubai, and Malta may also offer preferred routes.

Statistics from the Reserve Bank of India show that despite all the publicity around Bangalore, it received only about 7 percent of all FDI into India between 2000 and 2007. The areas surrounding Mumbai and Delhi each received about four times as much. Chennai fared about the same as Bangalore.

European companies have had a long history of success in India, whether ABB, Bayer, Bosch, Glaxo, SKF, Siemens, or Unilever. In the past, many international companies tended to follow the flag. "The entry of US companies in Asia was often aligned to oil trade and the Middle East or to the Philippines. At the same time, there was a political distaste for India's support of the nonaligned movement—or perhaps a sense that India was too friendly with communist countries. American companies had traditionally viewed India as an unfriendly place to do business," notes R. Gopalakrishnan of Tata Sons. But, he continues, "By the 1990s, the success of Indian immigrants in the United States demonstrated to corporate America the promise of Indian technical and managerial talent. Now global politics has shifted, and India and America are logical partners. American companies have a good future in India today."

One hundred percent investment is permitted in an ever-increasing number of sectors—although industries with limitations include defense, nuclear energy, multibrand retail, airlines, gambling and lotteries, insurance, and some aspects of media. Foreign companies with significant investments in India include cellular products company Nokia of Finland, drug maker GlaxoSmithKline of the UK, conglomerate Siemens of Germany, engineering firm ABB of Switzerland, carmaker Suzuki of Japan, steel giant Posco of South Korea, and American tech companies such as Cisco, Dell, General Electric, and IBM.

REMITTANCES

Emigrants and expatriates from India working in Persian Gulf countries, in North America, and in Western Europe sent $27 billion in remittances back home in 2007, according to World Bank estimates. India edged out Mexico and China as the largest recipient of such remittances and accounted for about 12 percent of global remittances. A sizable chunk of this inflow in hard currencies gets converted into Indian rupees and spent on family maintenance.

Foreign Institutional Investors

According to a Citigroup Research study released in September 2007, institutional investors from overseas held Indian equities that were valued at $193 billion and accounted for more than a fifth of the total holdings among the BSE 500 stocks. (The BSE 500 companies represent 93 percent of the capitalization on the Bombay Stock Exchange.)

FIIs, as they are called, began investing in India in January 1993, and there was a net outflow of investment only in fiscal year 1999. Since 2004, incoming investments rose sharply to above $10 billion per year, according to Reserve Bank numbers. Overseas investors include Fidelity, Janus, and Morgan Stanley from the United States; the government of Singapore via Temasek; European players such as UBS and HSBC; and many others.

Vivek Kudva is the president of Franklin Templeton Asset Management in Mumbai, and he is optimistic. Corporate India was historically dominated by family-owned business groups; now, however, the economic liberalization of the 1990s unleashed a new breed of companies that are professionally run and globally competitive. This has substantially widened the investment choices for institutional investors. Along the way, we have also seen substantial improvements in the corporate governance and the disclosure standards of Indian companies. This has coincided with the introduction of higher standards of corporate governance by the domestic regulator, and the growing influence of global investors, who expect an elevated degree of transparency in operations.

Joint Ventures

Many clients approach me to find or evaluate a joint-venture partner in India when they would be much better off with a vendor, distributor, or looser partnership agreement. In today's globalized world, both the Indian company and the foreign partner are liable to have multiple interests in multiple countries, and the relative alliances are likely to evolve over time. In this environment, it is important not to box yourself in to a joint-venture decision without some serious thought about other alternatives.

In a few industries, India actually requires foreign companies to engage with a joint-venture partner. In other cases, entrants to India seek local expertise with markets, government processes, or employee recruitment and retention. "One important criterion for a partner is a company with whom you can have an amicable divorce," asserts Arjun Malhotra, who co-founded Indian computer and services company HCL and went on to create joint ventures with Hewlett-Packard, Deluxe Corporation, and others.

The Tata group has participated in numerous joint ventures with American companies: Avaya, Timken, AIG, and others. R. Gopalakrishnan, who previously ran Unilever's India affiliate and is a Tata group board member, told me that he finds that there are two kinds of JV partners: those who want to partner for a while with a plan to buy out, and those who are interested in a long-term arrangement with no clear plan for exit. "American companies who want a long-term relationship have to determine if they are capable of sharing power. Some companies are genetically incapable of power sharing, and that can cause a long-term joint venture to falter."

Gopalakrishnan also states that foreign companies looking for a JV as a quick shortcut to enter the Indian market and then edge out the partner will have problems. "In the beginning of a relationship, clarity around management control is a key determinant of success." I couldn't agree with him more.

The Tata group has a strong fifty–fifty JV with Cummins, Inc.; both companies are true copilots in the entity. Since 1995, the company has produced about half a million low-emission diesel engines at a $75 million plant in Jamshedpur that employs about 850 people. But the Tatas had a different situation with IBM. "We had a friendly parting. We still continue to work very closely with IBM at numerous levels, but we both decided that Tata would exit the joint venture."

Michael Ducker of FedEx has been traveling to India for more than a decade, and his company has had experience with more than one agent/partner. His advice is to select your Indian partner carefully. First, make sure that you are aligned both strategically and operationally. Second, be clear about your objectives in India and ensure that you have a strong business case to be in India. Third, be a good corporate citizen in India from the start. You will need to develop government relations; you'll need local people to sort out problems and explain nuances of doing business. Finally, if you are just getting started, plan on making multiple trips to India. Take your time and do your research thoroughly.

ATTORNEY VISHAL GANDHI'S ADVICE ON JOINT VENTURES

Under Indian law, a joint-venture agreement does not bind the joint-venture company unless and until, in addition to being a party to the agreement, the key provisions of that agreement are incorporated in the articles of association of the JV company.

If the joint venture is with an Indian public company—even an unlisted one—the foreign partner should be aware that shares of an Indian public company are freely transferable per the 1956 Companies Act of India. Restrictions imposed on a joint-venture partner such as not transferring its shares to a competitor may not be enforceable. However, a remedy may still be available for breach of contract.

Care should be taken that the Indian joint-venture partner does not have authority to conclude contracts on behalf of the foreign partner. Otherwise, this may expose the foreign partner to adverse tax implications in India.

If any patents are being licensed to the Indian company by the foreign partner, it is a good idea for the foreign company to file for a patent in India first. If it does not, it may lose the right to patent in India.

India has no trade secrets law. So to protect its trade secrets, the American joint-venture partner should incorporate adequate and suitable provisions in the JV agreement. It is advisable that an American JV partner provides for arbitration in the agreement rather than providing for disputes to be submitted to the courts of a state in the United States, since US judgments are not necessarily easily enforceable in India.

Mergers and Acquisitions

Selling your company was a mark of both failure and disrespect in yesterday's India. Even today, many entrepreneurs are reluctant to buy or sell working businesses. But in the new India, more and more acquisitions are taking place in both directions. "Cross-border" or international deals continue to account for a significant portion of merger, acquisition, and strategic acquisition activity in India. Let's look at a few instances.

In 2007, London-based Vodafone set a record when it won approval from Indian regulators and Hutchinson Telecom shareholders to buy in to cell phone operator Hutch-Essar for $11.1 billion. A few months earlier, Oracle took control of software maker i-flex Solutions at a value of $600 million, and the world's third largest cement maker, Holcim, acquired a strategic state in Gujarat Ambuja Cements. Twenty-billion-dollar IT services company EDS Inc. expanded its stakes in India by acquiring a majority of Bangalore-based Mphasis for $380 million and all of test services vendor RelQ for about $40 million. OfficeTiger with principal operations in Chennai was purchased for $250 million in cash by printing giant RR Donnelley. In 2006, Kanbay—a North American company with significant operations in India—was acquired for $1.03 billion by CapGemini.

Indian companies, awash in profits and cash, have started to become bold about their own acquisitions and investments overseas. The world's fiftieth largest iron and steel firm, Tata Steel, used a leveraged buyout to acquire much larger Corus for $11.3 billion and vault into top ranks of steel companies worldwide. Shortly after this, Hindalco Industries purchased Novelis for $6.4 billion to become the world's largest aluminum-rolling entity. Tata Motors bought Jaguar and Land Rover, two venerable British brands. India's pharmaceutical companies Dr. Reddy's Labs and Ranbaxy have also made acquisitions exceeding $300 million each in Europe. Pune-based windmill company Suzlon Energy acquired Germany's Hansen group, a transmission maker, for $565 million and gained control of REpower, valued at $1.6 billion. Numerous other acquisitions of less than $100 million were driven by Indian companies looking to establish footholds in new markets or acquire key skills. Accounting firm Grant Thornton's *Dealtracker* newsletter reported that acquisitions by Indian companies grew from 28 in 2002 to 190 in 2006.

"Historically, Indians have been bolder in Europe and Asia than in North America," notes Guy Rabbat, who was on the board of GE India. "You can see that Vijay Mallya's Kingfisher paid $1.2 billion for Scotland-based Whyte and Mackay, and Laxmi Mittal bought Luxembourg-based Arcelor. So there's a more Indian–European kind of connection. Coming to America and acquiring is more difficult for an Indian company."

If you are planning to buy a company in India, it may help to get to know it well first. FedEx bought its Indian business partner after working with it for five years. Prakash Air Freight Express began domestic express operations in India in 1986, and has been the FedEx service provider in India since 2002. "We already knew them very well, so there were no surprises for us. We are now in the process of rebranding them as FedEx India, says Michael Ducker, president international of FedEx.

M&A is never easy, but if you are involved in a cross-border transaction with an Indian entity, whether as a buyer or a seller, there are three areas that need additional attention.

First, many traditional Indian companies may not keep books in the same way you might be familiar with. Some firms need to make legitimate payments in cash to vendors or employees, and to accept cash from clients. Others keep multiple sets of books, one for internal use and another for the government; the two sets may not be easy to reconcile. You may find that assessing the balance sheet of an older firm can be particularly challenging. For example, some listed assets may be worthless, while other valuable assets don't show up at all. Assigning fair values to these assets can also be hard, since you may not readily find comparable numbers. It is possible that your investigation may take longer than you expect and may not resolve all ambiguities.

Second, the regulatory and bureaucratic environment is almost never crystal clear. This is partly because vigorous global M&A is new to India; there are not a lot of precedents. Even with expert local guidance from bankers, accountants, and attorneys, you're likely to discover the application of some hitherto obscure or benign rule to your particular situation. Occasionally, such hiccups may be driven by a local competitor for the deal. Vodafone CEO Arun Sarin notes that, after he thought he had wrapped up the key points of his firm's acquisition of Hutch in India, reports began emerging of challenges to the process. "The billionaire losers' club was trying to unwind the deal. What I didn't count on was that the bureaucracy would kick in with this kind of evil spirit from our competitors who had lost." Don't rest easy until all aspects of the transaction are truly complete. This may take much longer than anyone first tells you. Don't start if you don't have the patience for a marathon that may distract you and your management team for a while.

Third, superb cross-cultural communication is crucial both during the transaction and upon its completion. The euphoria of a merger does not last long in a cross-border deal. All participants must prioritize the initiatives that require integration or collaboration and work diligently to overcome the cross-cultural challenges discussed in chapter 3.

Conclusion

A foreign company considering expanding business in India relative to emerging other economies should rarely have finance among its top worries. Capital is seldom in short supply for companies that want to enter or expand in today's India. Except in certain industries, money flows freely into and out of the nation. Among all the emerging economies of the early twenty-first century, India probably has the friendliest finance ecosystem for Western companies. You have many alternatives to raise and manage equity and debt, as well as working capital. Repatriation of profits is also fairly straightforward. You can count on domestic as well as Western finance partners being available for your needs.

CHAPTER 7

Key Legal and Accounting Issues

Before you make legal or accounting decisions relating to India, you should consult someone licensed to give advice on these subjects. This chapter gives you an overview of some business and pragmatic issues that might be helpful in such a discussion.

Courts and Arbitration

Much of the published material from Indian sources trumpets the fact that India and the United States share a foundation in English common law. They do, but this sometimes lulls Americans into a false sense of comfort. The first thing you should know is not to count on the Indian courts to deliver justice in a timely manner. "In America, it is convenient to use the law or contracts as a key business tool, and court justice comes relatively soon. But in India, it is better to do your homework carefully, since it can take a long time to get legal redress," cautions R. Gopalakrishnan, a board member at Tata Sons.

Washington, DC-based attorney Mark J. Riedy knows this from experience. He lived in India for several years and has won many legal actions there. For large contracts, he typically insists on a clause that guarantees third-country arbitration in a major dispute. In London, Paris, or Singapore, you can get resolution in twelve to twenty-four months, rather than in five to ten years in India. According to Riedy, "Courts move so slowly in India, if there was no new case in the Indian judicial system, it would take over 350 years to clear the backlog at the current pace." Riedy is an emeritus member of the board of the US–India Business Council (USIBC), an American trade group that works with business and government; he also serves as USIBC's general counsel.

In India, not only is the court system slow, but its speed is erratic and somewhat arbitrary. You could bring your whole team from overseas to argue a proceeding only to have the judge decide, with hardly any notice, that for some reason or another—vacation, illness—he or she is not going to hear the case. There is a significant expense to take that whole team back out of the country and then wait months or more before it comes up again.

While the Republic of India's constitution became effective on January 26, 1950, most laws that affect business were inherited from the legacy of British rule and carried over unchanged. At more than one hundred thousand words in the English version, it is the world's longest written constitution and has been amended over ninety times. Most federal laws in India apply to the entire country; the northern state of Jammu and Kashmir is sometimes treated as a special case.

India has just one Supreme Court, at the federal level, and it hears cases on constitutional issues and states' rights, as well as selected appeals from state High Court decisions. There is no equivalent, in India, to the American concept of federal courts. At the state level, the hierarchy is High Court, District Court, and the Court of Civil Judges (*munsifs*). There is no supreme court at the state level.

Few foreign companies need to raise issues at the Supreme Court. NYSE-listed News Corporation, run by Rupert Murdoch, is one of the few that have experienced India's Supreme Court. At a Milken Conference keynote speech in April 2007, Murdoch—whose wife, Wendi, is Chinese and helped launch MySpace China—lamented the difficulties he has had in doing business with China: "The fact is, media is pretty much closed." According to *The Hollywood Reporter,* however, he touted India as a good place to do business because its political structure at the top is "absolutely clean." He explained that News Corp. had taken two cases to the Indian Supreme Court and won both times. "It is a real, working democracy."

In 1996, India passed far-reaching updated legislation based on the United Nations Commission on International Trade Law's model laws. The Indian Arbitration and Conciliation Act recognizes foreign agreements and awards made under the 1961 New York convention.

Most foreign companies that resort to court action will find themselves starting at the District Court level. Decisions in these courts can take years and are often readily overturned by the state High Courts. There is much talk of judicial reform in India, and you will hear of efforts to computerize the judiciary, or to set up fast-track courts on a National Company Law Tribunal. But don't hold your breath.

Attorneys and Accountants

Don't make lawyer jokes in India; they're not relished by professionals in the same way they are in the United States. Attorneys are generally called advocates in India. Law school is typically two to three years; entry requires a bachelor's degree. Most law curricula in India are not as intense as in American schools. Many law school graduates do not ever practice law.

Also, unlike the United States, there is no state bar exam. An attorney with a degree recognized by the Bar Council of India can enroll with the appropriate state council, according to advocate Shantanu Surpure, who divides his time between Mumbai and California. In Mumbai only, an attorney may take a set of exams to qualify as a solicitor. The terms *barrister* and *vakil* are no longer used officially, but you may hear them used interchangeably with *advocate.*

Accountants in India typically have a bachelor's degree in commerce or accounting. The equivalent of a Certified Public Accountant (CPA) is called a Chartered Accountant (CA). Both industry experience as well as a special exam are requirements of the designation. CAs can often help with the paperwork you will encounter when starting a company in India.

Contracts

In the West, the legal contract often defines the essence of doing business. In India, as we have read in other chapters, the contract is important—but it is only a small part of the overall relationship between two parties. However, if you want the contract to be admissible in an Indian court, it must be executed on "stamp paper," which includes a "stamp duty" payment to the government. The cost of stamp duty can be large in the case of real estate transactions.

The Indian Contracts Act of 1872 was one of the British Crown's early decrees and is still operational, although specific types of contracts, such as partnerships and sales of goods, are now covered by more recent legislation. Compared with the United States, where practices in Louisiana may vary considerably from Delaware, most business people do not have to worry much about state-to-state variations in contract practices and law within India.

Transfer of Real Property

Real estate transactions in India are governed by the Transfer of Property Act of 1882. But titles are often murky. Records are rarely reliable and not available electronically, and the market is relatively illiquid. Not surprisingly, land is relatively expensive, and local presence can be a huge advantage when striking a real estate deal. Real estate transfers are now required to be registered; a substantial stamp tax is paid to the state government, ranging from 5 percent in Andhra Pradesh to almost 15 percent in Uttar Pradesh and Orissa.

Because Indian courts are backlogged with lawsuits relating to the transfer of property, it is not unusual for a case to drag on for decades until resolution; appeals then drag on for more decades. Thus, it will serve you well both to do your homework before entering into an agreement and to use high-quality advisers.

If you are involved in a real estate transaction with families in India, be aware of a practice that agreements made on account of love and affection, such as between brothers, or between parent and child, may be held to be enforceable even though no formal consideration is being exchanged. For example, if Jay Singh offers to sell you property that he earlier gifted to his brother Ram Singh for no consideration, you may find that you don't really have anything to buy.

Forms of Enterprise

Laws about forms of enterprise are consistent across India. So unlike the United States, you don't have to worry about whether to incorporate in Delaware or Nevada or your home state. The three primary forms of enterprise in India are proprietorships, partnerships, and companies.

The majority of small business people in India are sole proprietors. Except for some specific professions, an Indian citizen simply has to obtain an identification number (Personal Account Number or PAN) from the local office of the Income Tax Department, a federal agency. In practice, many micro-businesses do not register or pay income taxes. As a foreign company, you might require your vendors and business partners in India to provide evidence of registration.

Partnerships in India are governed by the 1932 Indian Partnership Act; partnership agreements are generally expressed in a written deed. Both companies and individuals can enter into a partnership. A Hindu Undivided Family (HUF) can also enter into a partnership through its leader or *karta*. It is not uncommon for a head of household in India to have adult married children and grandchildren living under the same roof and pooling all income and expenses. Indian law recognizes this "joint family" practice and gives it special consideration for income taxes.

Partnerships are not required to be registered; again, foreign companies may wish to require their business associates in India to provide evidence of registration. As with Western partnerships, any partner in India can act on behalf of the entire firm and bind it to a contract. Limited partnerships and limited liability partnerships don't yet exist in India, although Parliament has recently considered the idea.

Inspired by the Companies Act of the United Kingdom, the 1956 Companies Act in India regulates the creation and operation of domestic and foreign corporations. The law was amended considerably in 2000. The Registrar of Companies, often called the ROC, is a federal function with twenty-two offices throughout the country.

A private company in India must have a minimum capital investment of approximately $2,500, and the number of stockholders cannot exceed fifty. Private companies cannot raise equity or borrow money from the general public. You must have at least two directors in an Indian private company, unlike in the West where single-person companies are routine. Private-company shares are not transferable except as defined in its articles of incorporation. The government does not limit salaries or dividends paid to directors or employees of private companies. The name of a private company must have the words *Private Limited* appended—for instance, Conexant Systems India Private Limited.

A public company in India is any company that is not a private company, whether or not its stock is publicly traded. A public company must meet additional requirements such as having at least seven stockholders and three directors, having a paid-up capital investment of approximately $10,000, and having the salaries of its executives be restricted. A public company is permitted to raise capital or debt on the financial markets or via private arrangement and its shares may be sold freely or traded on a stock exchange. Of course, there are many additional requirements that an Indian public company must meet before it can hold a public stock offering and get listed. The Indian term *listed company* is roughly equivalent to the American term *publicly traded company.* Public companies are required to have the word *Limited* as part of their name, such as Colgate-Palmolive (India) Limited.

The term *promoter* in the United States is often associated with marketing or rock concerts. In twenty-first-
century India, you are likely to hear it in connection with
individuals who are putting together a company or a
building project. While the law does not require it, a foreign entity looking to promote a company in India should
probably use a local accountant or attorney to file papers
on its behalf.

WHAT'S THE PUBLIC SECTOR?

Though not defined in the Companies Act, you are likely to
hear the term *public-sector company* or *public-sector undertak-
ing* (PSU) in India. These are companies in which the federal
government and/or a state government is a major stockholder.
Even if 100 percent owned by a government, these entities are
required to follow the same company law practices as counterparts that have no government ownership. Their directors and
executive management are, of course, selected by the government.

The Indian government still controls most public-sector
companies, but several have risen to the top as the most valued companies in India and are traded on the Bombay Stock
Exchange. The Oil and Natural Gas Corporation, India's largest
multinational PSU, specializes in oil exploration and production. And the Indian Oil Corporation owns ten refineries, thirty
thousand retail outlets, and five thousand miles of pipeline.
Over 80 percent of the shares in both are owned by the Indian

government. Almost 90 percent of the National Thermal Power Corporation (which produces a quarter of India's electric power) is owned by the government. Through its Reserve Bank, the government controls 60 percent of India's largest bank, the State Bank of India.

Some of the largest and most visible companies in India are PSUs. Along the major roads, you will see gas stations with the name Indian Oil or Hindustan Petroleum; both are public-sector undertakings. India's flag carrier airline, Air India, is a PSU.

With liberalization, there was a move to privatize the PSUs. VSNL, a telecom and Internet service company, was sold to the Tata group. Modern Foods, a bakery, was sold to Unilever's India subsidiary. Stock in other entities was offered to the public. Privatization has slowed considerably in recent years. The federal government has flagged certain companies, called the Navratna (nine jewels) PSUs, which are considered too precious to "lose to" privatization. Not to be left behind, several other PSUs have since been granted the status of mini ratnas.

Note that many government undertakings do not take the form of a company. Among them are the Indian Railways with 1.6 million employees, which merits an entire ministry in the federal cabinet, and India Post, with 154,000 post offices and six hundred thousand employees under the ministry of Communications and Information Technology.

Forms of Enterprise for Foreign Companies

India's central bank, the Reserve Bank of India (RBI)—roughly equivalent to the Federal Reserve—is also tasked with managing the role of foreign companies in India.

For a short-term or tentative foray into twenty-first-century India, a foreign entity should consider creating a project office or liaison office. A liaison office needs RBI approval and can represent the foreign company in India, promote export and import, help establish technical and financial collaborations, and act as a communication channel between the parent and Indian companies. RBI prohibits the liaison office from charging fees or commissions and from actual trading; all of such an office's expenses must be paid through remittances from abroad. A project office is meant for a foreign company that has secured a contract in India and does not require RBI permission. Liaison and project offices of foreign companies are cost centers; since no revenue is attached to them, they are not subject to Indian income tax.

Some foreign companies find it expedient to set up a branch office in India, which requires specific approval from RBI. The approval also prescribes the activities that the branch office may undertake in-country. Unlike project and liaison offices, branch offices can actually buy and sell goods and services, in addition to simply *promoting* their purchase and sale. Transactions between the company and its India branch are subject to India's transfer pricing regulations. As you might expect, the Indian government is keen to earn and collect its share of taxes. Profits and unused funds at the branch can be readily repatriated with RBI approval. Branch offices can also meet their own expenses out of revenues generated in India and are subject to Indian income tax. Liability for activities of the branch office is transmitted back to the parent company, and branch offices are prohibited from manufacturing. Branch, liaison, and project offices do not require the foreign company to incorporate an Indian entity.

You may prefer to set up a subsidiary company or a joint venture with an Indian or foreign company in India. Such companies can raise capital on the Indian markets and can be treated as domestic Indian companies for tax purposes. The subsidiary or joint venture can be private or public. Most foreign entities that seek a long-term presence prefer to establish an Indian company sooner or later.

If you are not sure about your commitment to India, be cautious about setting up your Indian company. This is because liquidation and dissolution of a corporate entity is no trivial matter in India, even if the company had no operations whatsoever.

Intellectual Property Laws

As a founding member of the World Trade Organization, India has moved steadily to bring its laws into compliance with the Trade-Related Aspects of Intellectual Property Rights (TRIPS) Agreement. In 1999, it updated its Copyright Act to comply with the new developments in satellite broadcasting, computer software, and digital technology. Copyright registration is not generally required, and a sixty-year term is typically granted. Performers and their estates now hold copyright to recordings until fifty years after the performers' death.

The main problem with copyrights in India is not the laws themselves but their enforcement. As in much of Asia, you will find illegal copies of digital materials selling for pennies on the dollar. This includes Indian and Western movies, major software titles, and music. This is driven by small-scale pirates rather than the organized or state-sanctioned factories that have been written about in some other countries. Most companies of any size and most government departments now use only legal, licensed copies of products, if only to guard against disgruntled whistleblowers.

Fair-use exceptions to copyright law are significantly broader than American practices. This can affect entertainment companies as well as software development initiatives. In negotiating outsourcing contracts with Indian vendors, many attorneys add specific language prohibiting reverse engineering, copying, or reuse of software. This is probably a good idea. However, it is possible that some of these provisions could be overridden by the Indian fair-use doctrine in a court action.

A related issue around the use of independent contractors performing work for hire is significant. Unless contractor-created inventions are specifically assigned to the foreign client, Indian law accords the rights to such inventions and creations to the contractor who developed them and not to the foreign client. (Work performed by employees, on the other hand, belongs to the employer.)

India passed a new Trademarks and Merchandise Marks Act in 1999 and published compliancy rules three years later. A new Intellectual Property Appellate Board is head-quartered in Chennai; it also meets in Mumbai, Delhi, Kolkata, and Ahmedabad. The Patent Office is headquartered at Kolkata, with branches in Chennai, Delhi, and Mumbai. The Patents Act was most recently amended in 2005 and is TRIPS-compliant. Both product and process patents are permitted, each for a period of twenty years.

In 2005, *Time* magazine sued successfully in the Delhi High Court to prevent an Indian company from producing a magazine called *Time Asia Sanskaran*. The offending magazine also featured a cover with a distinctive red border matching the plaintiff's signature publication. For the first time in a case like this, the plaintiff was awarded punitive or exemplary damages. The judge, Justice R. C. Chopra, noted that the principle underlying punitive damages was to relieve the pressure on the criminal justice system by providing a civil alternative to criminal prosecution for minor crimes. Another example of this is that, while Zippo cigarette lighters are not sold in India, Justice H. R. Malhotra of the Delhi High Court issued an injunction in October 2006 against a rival company whose product had the same distinctive shape as the plaintiff's products.

Computer programs are not currently patentable under Indian law. This is a worry for many Western companies outsourcing or offshoring work to India.

INTELLECTUAL PROPERTY RIGHTS ARE A TWO-WAY STREET

Western companies would be wise to recognize that the patent controversy cuts both ways. There was considerable backlash in India when American entities attempted to patent what was seen in India as traditional knowledge. In 1992, W. R. Grace & Co. was granted a US patent on Neemix, a pesticide whose active ingredient is found in the seeds of the neem tree, which grows all over India and whose beneficial properties have been common knowledge in India for thousands of years. Lawsuits filed in Europe and the United States accused Grace of "bio-piracy"; the firm ended up selling the product rights to another company.

In a similar fashion, the University of Mississippi was briefly granted a US patent in 1995 on the use of turmeric to augment the healing of chronic and acute wounds. This process has been also widely known in India for hundreds of years, and turmeric is a common spice found in most Indian households. The patent was revoked.

Ricetec, Inc., of Alvin, Texas, caused an uproar in India when it was granted a patent named "Basmati Rice Lines and Grains" in 1997 for the famous aromatic Indian rice called basmati, which the firm cross-bred with a local long-grained rice. Ricetec eventually withdrew fifteen of its twenty claims and changed the name of its patent to "Rice Lines Bas867, RT 1117, and RT1121."

In addition to inventions, the patent office in India is also charged with protecting "designs" under a 2000 revision. The term *industrial designs* refers to creative activity that results in the ornamental or formal appearance of a product. A separate law administered by the Ministry of Communications and Information Technology protects designs relating to semiconductor circuits.

Employment Laws

India is a member of the International Labor Organization. A number of laws apply to blue-collar and white-collar employment; to the payments of wages, bonuses, and "gratuity"; to maternity benefits; to industrial disputes; and more. If you have employees in India, you will need an Indian accountant to advise you on your responsibilities relating to these laws. A high-level summary follows. Bear in mind that not all laws apply to all companies, and there are numerous nuances that are not explained below.

The 1936 Payment of Wages Act applies mostly to factory workers and seeks to ensure that they get paid on time, and that no unauthorized deductions are taken from their wages. The Industrial Employment Act of 1946 now applies to most establishments of more than fifty workers and regulates their working conditions, holidays, shifts, vacations, and termination. Some Indian entrepreneurs try to circumvent its provisions by capping employment at just under that ceiling and creating additional companies to hire new employees. Western companies are well advised not to try such devices. The 1948 Minimum Wages Act determines base-level rates for certain occupations specified in schedules; in practice most Western companies will exceed those minimums by a considerable margin.

The Industrial Disputes Act, passed in 1947, provides for the investigation and settlement of lockouts, layoffs, strikes, and retrenchment. Managers, supervisors, and most professional employees are not covered by this law. Requirements are more onerous than in the United States. A worker who has been employed for more than a year must be given one month's written notice or pay in lieu thereof; in addition, the workman must also be given fifteen days' pay for each year of service. The Workmen's Compensation Act of 1923 is similar to laws in the United States. But the kind of organized fraud seen in the US between corrupt attorneys and physicians working with employees who pretend to get hurt is hardly heard about in India.

The 1965 Payment of Bonus Act applies to companies with more than twenty employees and provides for additional payments based on productivity, production, or profits. Even if the company runs a loss in any year, a minimum "bonus" of 8.33 percent, or one month's wages, for employees is required. The nearest equivalent to Social Security in India is called Provident Fund; by law, employees and employers contribute matching amounts of around 10 to 12 percent of the salary. Employees can choose to contribute more if they wish.

The 1972 Payment of Gratuity Act requires significant payments to employees when they retire, resign, are terminated, are disabled, or die. Gratuity is calculated at the rate of fifteen days' pay for every year of service. For this reason the word *gratuity* seldom implies "tip" in India.

Consumer Protection

While India has not seen huge legal damage awards to aggrieved consumers, a foreign company should be especially careful with laws and practices relating to consumer protection.

For example, in October 2007, British Airways was ordered to pay about $13,000 to an elderly woman who was stranded at Heathrow Airport for five days on her way to New Delhi. The incident happened in 2003. In April 2007, a software drink bottler was fined about $2,500 five years after a consumer reported a foreign object in one of its bottles. Bad publicity is a valid concern, perhaps as much as the legal implications for many companies in this situation.

The 1986 Consumer Protection Act regulates the activities of any manufacturer or service provider that delivers products or services to consumers. Commercial and industrial buyers that purchase goods for resale are excluded from protection under this law. The law created county-level Consumer Disputes Redressal Forums, which can resolve disputes of up to about $50,000. State-level forums can address claims up to five times that amount; beyond this level, claims must be referred to the National Consumer Dispute Redressal Forum.

These bodies have the power to require the supplier to repair or replace a defective product or refund the price paid. They also have the power to award compensation for loss or injury to the individual. Further, the bodies have the power to order the withdrawal of hazardous products and the discontinuance of a trade practice deemed unfair or restrictive.

One other law relating to consumer protection is significant: the Right to Information Act. Today, for a fee of 25 cents, an Indian citizen can petition the public information officer at any government department for information. This landmark law, passed in 2005, applies to all federal and state government departments and to nongovernmental organizations (NGOs) funded substantially by the government. Petitioners do not have to give a reason for their request, and the department is required to provide an answer in thirty days.

There are a few limitations on the information that can be sought under this act, such as information that would affect the sovereignty and integrity of the country and information protected by commercial confidence, trade secrets, or intellectual property. Select government agencies, in functions such as intelligence and security, are excluded from most provisions of the act, but they are still required to provide information relating to human rights violations.

While most success stories under the act have to do with personal and citizenship issues, such as getting electric utilities fixed, voter ID cards corrected, and pension requests fulfilled, foreign companies may find that the act can be helpful to their Indian employees.

Accounting and Taxes

The Indian fiscal year runs from April 1 to March 31 of the following year. Contrary to American practice, Indian balance sheets show assets on the right side. Liabilities and owners' equity are shown on the left. As we saw in an earlier chapter, Indians count in thousands, lakhs, and crores. One hundred thousand makes up one lakh; one hundred lakhs is a crore. So 2.5 million rupees is written as 25,00,000 and called twenty-five lakhs. With these exceptions, financial statements from India are generally similar to Western ones.

Most company records have to be audited externally. The big global accounting firms have corresponding offices in India; there are plenty of Indian firms with no Western affiliation as well.

All listed companies in India are required to have a "company secretary" on staff. This senior executive is responsible for corporate compliance and governance issues. Company secretaries in India are responsible for corporate conduct at board and stockholder meetings, communication with stockholders, compliance, regulatory and listing requirements, administration of real property contracts, and sometimes insurance, pensions, and benefits administration.

Despite liberalization, India has more kinds of taxes and

higher taxes than most countries. Vast ministries at the state and federal levels have hundreds of thousands of employees devoted to administering, collecting, monitoring, and auditing taxes.

Individuals who earn more than a certain threshold pay a progressive federal income tax, which caps out at under 34 percent. (In 1974, the maximum incremental income tax was 97.5 percent!) There is no individual state income tax, but certain states impose a profession tax on certain professions. Like the United States, India taxes worldwide income. Talk to a tax specialist about credits for double taxation if you are a foreigner living and working in India for more than ninety days. Note that India now taxes most "fringe" benefits paid to employees; also, long-term capital gains are taxed at lower rates (much as in the US)— typically 20 percent. Dividends, whether declared, distributed, or paid, are taxed at almost 17 percent. Corporate income is taxed at about 34 percent for domestic companies and 42 percent for foreign companies.

Customs duties on most imported goods were reduced during liberalization. But the effective duty is layered: Basic customs duty peaks at 12.5 percent. In addition, there is usually a countervailing duty to match the amount of excise tax that an Indian manufacturer might pay. This might run at an additional 16 percent. Two additional duties are charged on top of this. The first—uncreatively named "additional duty"—is equivalent to the sales tax that a local vendor might pay; it is usually either 4 or 12 percent. There is also an "educational cess" of 3 percent on top of the tax. Dizzy? Talk to your customs agent or accountant.

On goods manufactured in India there is a central excise duty, now called "cenvat," of about 16.48 percent of the value added. Most states have replaced the state sales tax with a state value-added tax. If you sell services in India, you are required to pay services tax.

Most changes to federal taxes are announced in the union budget by the finance minister, typically on the last day of February. The complete budget is posted online at the same time.

This is not a complete list of all taxes. There are also many exceptions and variations. Penalties for noncompliance are unpleasant. Consult your local experts and ask them to keep you apprised of updates, changes, incentives, and ethical loopholes.

Conclusion

As long as you have sound professional guidance—and you don't expect quick resolution from Indian courts—you should be able to devote most of your energy to running your business rather than dealing with procedural matters or red tape. Prior to liberalization, it would have been difficult to make such a statement.

CHAPTER 8

Traveling There and Living There

Given urban overcrowding and tighter interpersonal-space preferences than the West, India can appear unfriendly and overwhelming to the visitor at first. Indeed, many Indians might seem rude or uncaring toward strangers. This is primarily because many people do not trust strangers and will generally apply the same yardstick to foreigners as they do to compatriots whom they do not know. In addition, you may find that unsolicited "help" from strangers in public places comes from those who want to benefit from you commercially. However, other offers of help may be quite well intentioned with nothing overt expected in return. Most business people who are seasoned international travelers can tell hustlers from helpers fairly quickly. If you are unsure, be polite, smile slightly, thank the stranger, and decline the offer; but don't feel that you have to part with your money or your time.

To a first-time visitor from the United States, India can

feel like Superman's "Bizarro" world. Indians drive on the wrong side of the road, electrical appliances take 220 volts at 50 hertz instead of the American 110 volts at 60 hertz, the on–off switches work backward, the plugs are the wrong shape, accounting balance sheets show liabilities on the left side rather than the right, deals are counted in lakhs and crores rather than millions or billions . . . even the time zone is offset to five and a half hours before Greenwich Mean Time.

It's easy to react negatively on first impressions, and I urge our clients to withhold final judgment for a few days. That's because you might actually change your mind if you keep yourself open to new ways of looking at the world. If you manage people who might be required to travel or relocate to India, it is reasonable to assume that some percentage of your staff just won't be able to handle the transition. Reluctant business travelers or expatriates will often harden their mind-sets about the poverty, the heat, the traffic, the disease, the noise, the overpopulation, or whatever it is that irks them about the country, and it may not be worthwhile putting them in a situation that hampers their productivity.

A different India emerges below that veneer. Mason Byles can never forget the kindness and generosity of people at all levels of Hindustan Computers Ltd. (HCL) near Delhi in north India, where he spent two years working; his company, Hewlett-Packard, was the minority joint-venture partner. "People went out of their way to make sure that I was okay," he reminisces. Joe Sigelman traveled to many developing countries as a child and remembers protesting at age twelve, "I could never live in India . . ." Fate brought him back to south India as an adult, and after spending seven years in Chennai, he now exclaims, "There are few countries in the world that would have welcomed a foreigner the way India has for me and, for that, I am going to be forever grateful."

Traveling to India

In 2006, a vice president at a $600 million company in the Midwest who had attended one of my speeches approached us. He and his three immediate reports had planned a trip to India. But only *one* of the dozen or so India companies that his staff contacted had responded to their e-mails and phone calls. Upon research and analysis, we found that they were saying the wrong things to the wrong people, and at least five of the best prospects in India were not even on their list. By using in-country resources, we were quickly able to identify and correct these issues and help them to plan an effective investigative trip.

If your company is engaging India for the first time, it is wise to use a trusted adviser or consultant who is familiar with business in the nation today. Prospective Indian vendors or customers may ignore your initial overtures if you approach them on your own. Often this is because they have previously been burned by casual inquiries from the West that resulted in no business. Also, in a growing economy, many Indian companies are prospering to the point that they are picky about whom they do business with, yet they are not culturally comfortable with telling you no, so they may just ignore your inquiry or give you a muted noncommittal response. Worse, you may get positive responses from companies that are ill matched, immature, or so poorly run that they don't have enough prospective customers. Do your homework before you make that expensive trip.

Tim Lenihan, an electrical engineer from Colorado, has visited India fifteen times and has found that meetings should be set up well in advance. "Many e-mails do not get responded to, or it may be weeks before a response arrives. It is better to call the person if you know them or use a knowledgeable contact to set up an introduction, which can lead to a meeting."

Planning a Business Trip

India is nine to twelve time zones away from North America, and business-class airfare generally runs more than $8,000. While there are now a few nonstop flights to Delhi and Mumbai from Chicago and from the New York area, it is still at least eighteen hours from your home to the hotel at your first destination in India. For this reason alone, trips of less than a week in duration are generally too stressful to be productive.

You may suffer extreme jet lag upon arrival. Many travelers find that mild medications such as melatonin are insufficient to cope with the time change. You may want to ask your doctor for a prescription sleep aid such as Ambien or a generic equivalent like zolpidem. Most seasoned travelers adjust their watches as soon as they arrive at the departing airport and try to avoid sleep on touching down in India until it is nighttime there.

You must have your passport stamped with a visa from the Indian embassy or consulate designated for your home address. (If you live in Canada or another country that is a part of the British Commonwealth, the Indian embassy in your country is called a High Commission.) This process takes a few days, and you must follow very specific guidelines listed on the embassy Web site. In the United States, the Indian embassy began outsourcing the visa application process to Travisa Outsourcing, Inc., in October 2007. Your company may have a travel agent or specialized third party that handles the visa process. It is a good idea to apply for a ten-year visa if the appropriate consulate will permit you to do so. If you were born in Pakistan or hold a Pakistani passport, you can expect additional scrutiny regardless of your current citizenship or place of residence. People of Indian origin may find it worthwhile to apply for overseas citizenship of India, if applicable to them. While its benefits are limited, it does facilitate travel to India.

When I travel to India, I scan my passport, visa, travel itinerary, and any other papers, then e-mail the resulting files to my Web-mail address. This way, if I do lose any such important documents or my computer while traveling, I can go to any internet café and print out copies readily. I also pack a few extra passport-size photographs; you may need them on short notice in India.

If you wish to receive immunizations and begin pro-phylactic malaria medications prior to your trip, consult the Web site for the Centers for Disease Control for cur-rent recommendations in advance of visiting your local health care facility. You should pack at least two bottles of mosquito repellent and always carry one on your person. You might find mosquitoes in an office restroom or on a tourist bus.

Make hotel reservations, business appointments, and intra-India travel reservations in advance—but schedule yourself lightly on your first trip. Unexpected opportuni-ties and unanticipated problems will likely spring up. You will no doubt find yourself juggling your schedule while you are in-country.

You will need a working cell phone, and most GSM carriers, such as AT&T, T-Mobile, and Sprint, work well in India, although roaming charges can be stiff. If your phone is from a CDMA carrier, such as Verizon, you should check with the carrier to confirm where and whether your hand-set is guaranteed to work; you may need to buy a special phone. It is often helpful to have an Indian cell phone number while you are there, since many native trades-people will hesitate to call you on an international num-ber. You can rent mobile phones with Indian numbers at most international airports.

If you are in India for several days, you can also buy prepaid mobile phone service; you'll need to show your passport, offer a verifiable local address, and have at least two passport-size photos. Security concerns with cellular usage are crucial in India, so you cannot simply pick up a SIM card anonymously. For that reason, you should also not lend your Indian phone to a stranger or, worse, *sell* your SIM card for unused minutes at a local phone store. Prepaid phones can be readily refilled by the bell desk at any major hotel, at designated carrier stores, as well as at retail shops across the cities. However, refills from general stores are usually small-denomination and may not apply if you bought your phone service in a different city.

Airlines, Hotels, and Cars

Many Indian airports, including Delhi and Mumbai, have separate domestic and international terminals—and they are *not* located within walking distance. If you need to switch to a domestic flight upon arriving from overseas, check the details on switching terminals ahead of time. Both Mumbai and Delhi airports have been privatized recently and will undergo considerable construction and reconfiguration in the next several years.

On your first trip to India, it is best to have your hotel pick you up or have some other arrangement to "receive" you upon arrival. Services like Avis also provide clean, reliable, chauffeur-driven cars at the major airports. Taking a commercial (yellow and black) taxi is the last resort; should you need to do so, look for the prepaid taxi counter inside the baggage claim area, where you can pay a flat rate in rupees depending on your destination. This way you don't have to worry about an unscrupulous driver giving you an unsolicited grand tour of the city immediately upon your arrival. These taxis may not be very clean and the drivers may not speak English.

If you need to fly within India, you will find most airports to be antiquated and overcrowded. Air traffic is increasing rapidly, in fact the Mumbai–Delhi air route was ranked sixth busiest in the world by the Official Airline Guide in 2007. Jetways are rare, ceilings are low, and even the business-class lounges are noisy, besides being on the outside of security. Security staff are curt but efficient. But once you are airborne on a carrier such as Jet Airways (not Jet Lite) or Kingfisher, get ready for a full meal with real cutlery, moist towelettes at takeoff and landing, and polite, attentive service. If you are in business class—and I highly recommend that you buy discounted business-class coupons overseas before you enter the country—you will get personal attention that rivals top global carriers, such as Singapore Airlines. The fact that these Indian carriers can offer such levels of service despite the chaos and confusion on the ground is one of those miracles that can apparently only happen in India. The only other domestic carrier that I let my clients fly on in India is state-owned Air India (which recently took over sibling Indian Airlines), primarily because of its large network. More than a dozen other airlines have sprung up—Deccan (recently acquired by Kingfisher), SpiceJet, Go, Indigo, and more. Some of these are no-frills carriers, and others don't yet have enough history or financial muscle for me to be comfortable recommending them.

At the top hotels in India, you will generally receive much better personal service than you might experience in other parts of the world, especially in North America. This includes properties with Western names such as Hilton, Hyatt, and Starwood, as well as Indian chains including Oberoi and Taj. For example, on a recent trip, I called housekeeping at the Grand Maratha (a Starwood property) in Mumbai at 11:30 PM to tell them that my Indian cell phone plug would not fit properly in the desk socket. They immediately sent an electrician to reverse the direction of the three-pin plug; he was done in fifteen minutes. Be aware that prices at four- and five-star hotels match or exceed top hotels in New York or London.

Service at the next tier of hotels can range from almost as good to very spotty. Minimal-service business hotels with names like Ginger and Lemontree have sprung up lately that are more affordable and more predictable.

Most three-star and better hotels have clean comfortable beds, full backup power, twenty-four-hour air-conditioning (although your room lights and a/c may automatically turn off when you leave the room), and Western-style toilets, where you don't have to squat.

Once you go below the three-star level anywhere in India, you have to be watchful about comfort, food safety, and predictability. Business travelers with limited time in India should get specific local guidance about the current service levels and toilets at any such property before committing to stay there.

Television shows on the National Geographic Channel and PBS romanticize the state-owned Indian Railways. But filthy, hot stations, inadequate signage, unreliable food hygiene, and more can make it challenging for a business traveler to get much value from using intercity trains, unless accompanied by a local person. Trains such as the Palace on Wheels in Rajasthan and the Taj Express to Agra can make for an interesting weekend diversion, but in most cases business travelers will find it easier to use a combination of air and road transport.

The Delhi Metro rail is presently the only world-class urban commuter system in India, with air-conditioned coaches, well-marked stations, and modern ticketing. It generally won't throw foreign business visitors for a loop. Kolkata has a limited underground train that is being expanded, and there are commuter systems under construction in Bangalore and Hyderabad as well.

To get to most destinations within a city or to travel to nearby cities within two hundred miles of your hotel, you will probably want to rent a chauffeur-driven car. The better car services provide uniformed drivers who speak some English and carry mobile phones. Prices vary dramatically from city to city and by make of car. Don't even consider driving on your own as a business visitor to India. Be ready for some hair-raising experiences as your driver appears to career through the chaotic traffic using his horn more than his brakes. Wear your seat belt and insist that your driver does likewise. Indian laws and common sense dictate this use. Older cars may not have belts in their rear seats, but you will encounter those only in smaller cities or noncommercial situations. If the driver appears to speed unsafely on a clear stretch of road, don't hesitate to tell him firmly to slow down.

"Every car or truck has on its bumper a sign that proclaims PLEASE BLOW HORN," chuckles Bob Nichols, vice president at Tempel Steel, which has operations in Chennai. "In driving on these roads, you would think that you would see more accidents, but you do not. Ideally you must drive in the biggest SUV, sit in the backseat, buckle up, close your eyes, and wish for the best."

Women Travelers

Women occupy positions of power in all kinds of Indian companies, so female travelers here won't feel out of place. If you are a woman traveling with a group of male Western colleagues, you may want to assert and define your role and responsibility clearly early on so that everyone on the Indian side takes you seriously. If a traditional Indian man appears to ignore you, it might well be that he is unsure how to speak with you. It is okay to break the ice with a simple question or comment. And don't be surprised if he addresses you as "madam"! In India, that is the respectful way to speak to a lady.

You are well advised to dress somewhat conservatively, avoiding plunging necklines, short skirts, and sleeveless blouses in most business situations. If you have seen more daring dresses in Bollywood movies, remember that they are just movies; also, standards vary from city to city and company to company. Women do travel alone on business in India, but you may want to avoid low-end hotels. A few higher-end hotels offer secured women's wings, where unaccompanied men are not allowed. You may also find ladies' sections on trains and in some restaurants. In some situations there are separate, shorter, more civilized lines for women, or women may be allowed to jump to the front of an all-male line.

In smaller cities, women who smile a lot and appear very friendly may attract undesired attention from men. Typically, it is from men who are not used to dealing with Western women, and their "understanding" of foreign women may come from television shows like *Baywatch.*

If you want to endear yourself to your Indian hosts, try donning a few items of Indian clothing or jewelry. While a saree is too intimidating for most first-time visitors, necklaces, earrings, bracelets, bangles, or scarves are easy. If you are a trifle more adventurous, try a salwar-kameez. (A kameez is a loose-fitting long-sleeved blouse that comes down past the waist; salwar are loose-fitting trousers, wide at the top and narrow at the ankles.)

Minorities

Indians talk about religion, politics, color, and ethnicity quite freely at work, and lighthearted humor on these subjects is not considered politically incorrect. So if you are Chinese American, African American, Jewish with a yarmulke or ringlets, you should expect questions about your appearance and the role of your ethnic group in American society. Many Indians don't see this as rude or intrusive, even in a work situation. To them it is just as normal as asking if you are a Yankee or a Red Sox fan. To the extent that you are comfortable, you should answer these questions, at least briefly.

Lonnie Sapp, who is African American, moved to Chennai at a time when there were very few Americans living there, and almost no African Americans. He advises minorities, especially African Americans, to leave any preconceived notions of racism behind. In America, minorities must compete on many levels and overcome color-based biases. But in India, he didn't feel any of this type of pressure. "In fact, my color was an advantage in my opinion," he says with a smile. "Yes, I was a foreigner, but some of the employees felt more comfortable with me because of my complexion." He also suggests that individuals who are planning to relocate or simply traveling on business should try to learn some of the local language and customs.

People with Disabilities

Buildings in India are not generally designed to be wheelchair-friendly; neither are toilets. Sidewalks may be uneven, and crosswalks generally don't have ramps. You might consider hiring a helper when you travel in India if you have a physical disability.

Gays and Lesbians

Laws against homosexuality that were promulgated during British rule are still on the books in India. These laws are seldom enforced but have served to keep most gay and lesbian activity in the shadows. While there are active gay movements in Mumbai, Delhi, and some other cities, many Indians don't understand gay or lesbian orientation. If you wish to reach out to the gay or lesbian community in India, it's probably wisest to make contact over the Internet ahead of your arrival.

Incidentally, same-gender physical contact in public is quite common among heterosexuals in India. Foreigners new to India may sometimes assume that grown men walking hand-in-hand in a shopping mall are gay, but that would be wrong.

Staying Safe

Use your mosquito repellent liberally and always carry it with you; you may need it aboard a bus, in a restroom, even in some offices. While you can take medications to protect against malaria, the protection is never 100 percent. Besides, mosquitoes carry other very unpleasant diseases such as dengue fever and chikungunya virus. Not every bite results in sickness, so don't get alarmed if you do get bitten, but report any fever, rash, or other conditions to a doctor.

If you want to avoid "Delhi Belly," drink only bottled water and carry a bottle with you at all times. To be safe, stick with mainstream brands, like Kinney or Aquafina, bought from mainstream locations such as your hotel or larger stores. Make sure the lid is sealed. Ice can be just as dangerous as water and is best avoided. Also steer clear of uncooked vegetables or fruit that can't be peeled. It's probably a good idea to carry Pepto-Bismol, Mylanta, or your favorite antacid with you, in case you do get an upset stomach.

As a business traveler, your other risk is a traffic accident. Many cars sold in India would be called subcompacts in the West and don't offer much protection in the event of an accident. Renting something heavier, such as an SUV (a Chevrolet Tavera or the like), a mini van (say, a Toyota Inova), or at least a "larger" sedan (such as a Toyota Corolla or Honda Citi) gives you a little more metal around yourself. And while many Indians don't bother with seat belts when sitting in the rear seat, you should always buckle up.

When you are a pedestrian, remember that might is right in India, and the pedestrian is at the bottom of the pecking order. Cross streets carefully, watching not only for cars and trucks but also for bicycles, three-wheelers, and in some cities the occasional horse-drawn cart or stray cow.

There is some street theft in any major city, so it is best to hang on to your purse or wallet in public places. In general, though, there is little danger to your physical safety in India.

DINNER WITH A STRANGER

On one trip to Rajasthan, I was very close to the India–Pakistan border, and the local In-Tourist guide asked me what sites I wanted to see. His job was to guide me to the local tourist attractions. Having seen dozens of temples, forts, shrines, and historical buildings, I said I would really like to meet the people of Rajasthan. Without hesitation, he invited me to his house for dinner.

When I left the hotel it was dark, and I took a scooter-taxi (a three-wheeled vehicle, also called a tuk-tuk in other countries) to his address. The neighborhoods we passed got poorer and poorer, and the darkness increased with the decreasing number of streetlights. I thought to myself, perhaps this wasn't such a good idea—the In-Tourist guide was a complete stranger and I wouldn't have been able to find my way back to the hotel through the maze of streets. We arrived at a two-story concrete dwelling and the In-Tourist guide greeted me at the door. It was clear he was just scraping by with a large family. He was the only one who spoke English. We went through the downstairs and up onto the roof.

Because we were in the middle of a desert, the night sky was absolutely clear. His wife and daughter brought the dinner to the roof, and we had a wonderful meal under the stars. We talked about Rajasthan and why it is unique in India and about India in general. It is an experience I will not forget. I was impressed with his willingness to share what little he had with a

complete stranger. He arranged for a scooter to take me back to the hotel; my nervousness was unwarranted.
—Tim Lenihan, Colorado

Food and Dining

Most so-called Indian restaurants in the West serve Punjabi food such as naan bread and tandoori chicken. Regional cuisine from Gujarat, Tamil Nadu, Kerala, Bengal, even Uttar Pradesh can be completely different from Punjabi food. Most Indian food is spicy, even when you ask for a mild version. Chinese restaurants are popular in India, although the cooking acquires a distinctly Indian spicy veneer. And don't be shocked if you see Indians smothering their chow mein or pizza with chili sauce or ketchup. Most Indian desserts are made from dairy products, and milk, yogurt, or cream are ingredients to many entrée recipes; if you are lactose intolerant you should not hesitate to ask a lot of questions about the food you are offered.

In a city like Mumbai or Delhi, you can find most international cuisine, "except Mexican" according to Mark Bullard, who moved to Mumbai from Bentonville, Arkansas, and misses his fajitas and tacos. High-end hotels usually house several top-quality restaurants that attract locals. For example, Bukhara—listed among *Restaurant* magazine's global top fifty—is inside the Maurya hotel in Delhi and also has a branch inside another hotel in Mumbai.

After a few days, some Americans find that they need their fix of McDonald's, KFC, Subway, or Domino's Pizza. These chains have outlets in major Indian cities. There are some Indian restaurant chains such as Nirula's in Delhi or Only Parathas in Mumbai that are clean, efficient, and worth trying. Starbucks addicts will miss their favorite brand, but India has three successful chains that sell premium coffee and snacks: Barista Coffee, Costa Coffee, and Café Coffee Day. At most Indian fast-food restaurants, you will find a station to charge the battery on your cell phone, with an assortment of connectors. Business travelers on short trips should avoid roadside restaurants and pushcart vendors, since their hygiene practices can vary.

Some restaurants in India serve only vegetarian fare. When an Indian says, "I don't eat meat," he or she includes fish, chicken, and mollusks in addition to beef, pork, or lamb. Others will eat dairy and egg products and may refer to themselves as "eggetarians." Restaurants are often called "hotels" in India. In Tamil Nadu, where many restaurants are vegetarian, "military hotel" is code for an eating place that serves nonvegetarian food.

Most visitors enjoy beer brewed in India, such as Kingfisher, although it can be stronger than the American version. Indian-Made Foreign Liquor (IMFL) such as whiskey, rum, and gin may not appeal to visitors' palates. Imported alcohol is available, and scotches such as Chivas Regal and Johnnie Walker are quite popular but fairly expensive relative to IMFL. A few good Indian wines have emerged in recent years, but most Indians are not avid wine drinkers.

With the exception of cashew feni in Goa and perhaps coconut toddy in some coastal areas, you are unlikely to find good "country liquor" at any restaurant that might be safe for you to eat at.

You don't have to learn complicated rules and rituals around dining in India. Most Indians won't take food from another person's plate or drink from someone else's glass, since your germs are supposed to have polluted your food and plate. Many Indians prefer to eat with their hands rather than knives and forks. Traditionally, the left hand was considered unclean, but in the new India this is not a factor; you may get a few giggles if you eat with your left hand, but little else.

Breakfast meetings are rare in India, and dinner is often eaten very late in the evening. At an Indian party, most socializing happens before dinner, and guests often leave immediately after dessert, which could be served as late as midnight.

Health Care

While the majority of Indians have very limited access to medical services, as a business traveler or expatriate you will find very affordable high-quality care available in most cities. Doctors and hospitals may expect to be paid immediately for their services, but fees are reasonable, and you can always claim after-the-fact reimbursement from your Western plan, if appropriate.

Bring copies of all your prescriptions for medications,

eyeglasses, and hearing aids with you, and make sure you know the generic names of any prescription medications. If you are taking medications that were introduced in the last decade or so, it is best to inquire from your own physician about alternatives, in case the drug maker has not yet offered the particular item in India. Conversely, you may find that some treatments not yet approved by American or European authorities are being offered in India. A friend of mine needed a sudden angioplasty in Chennai a few years ago, and physicians installed an advanced stent that the FDA did not approve for American use for another twenty-four months.

Medical privacy is not a given in India. The examination room may double as the doctor's office, and the partitions from the patient waiting area may not be quite soundproof. Many Indians have a very deferential attitude toward their physicians, and you may find the bedside manner of Indian physicians to vary from extremely courteous to almost imperious. Older physicians are often not accustomed to patients who question them. I suggest accompanying your queries with a disarming smile.

If you do get sick on a short trip to India, resist the tendency to wait until you return home before you see a doctor. Local doctors are most familiar with local bugs and their treatment. What might be a ten-minute diagnosis in India can drag on to a multiweek affair back home if you catch something that your physician or lab is not familiar with.

Western medicine is called allopathy in India. Several

forms of alternative medicine are quite popular. If you spend any length of time in India, you are sure to encounter homeopathic medicine, which originated in Germany in the nineteenth century but is practiced more widely in India than in most other countries. Other common alternative medical systems include ayurveda, which originated in India; unani, which came to India by way of Persia; and naturopathy. It is beyond the scope of this book to comment on the efficacy of any of these systems, but you should be aware that all are practiced widely, and India is one of the few countries that grants official recognition to these systems. You may want to verify the kind of medicine practiced by a particular physician before making an appointment. You will also find many Indians who swear by the efficacy of these alternative systems; in fact, some allopathic physicians may occasionally prescribe alternative therapies.

Managing India from Afar

While circumstances may drive you to start by managing your India operation from afar, once it has developed scale, it should be managed by someone who lives there.

If a Western company assigns India to third-country executives who are not well versed in today's India, they can count on serious pushback or passive resistance from Indian employees; it is often unwise for an American company to have India managed out of Singapore, Dubai, Sydney, or Hong Kong.

If you are going to manage from North America or Europe, plan on starting your workweek on Sunday night and stagger your schedule to overlap some of your workdays with those of your Indian colleagues. You may need to travel to India for a few weeks every quarter. You may also want to have your direct reports travel to you several times a year.

Despite videoconferencing, instant messaging, and conference calling, you will likely find that managing your India operation from afar can only be a stopgap measure.

Living in India

I remember one day getting off the airplane for the first time in 1999. I took an auto-rickshaw from the airport to the Taj Connemara Hotel in Chennai in Tamil Nadu. I went to the receptionist and asked for the long-stay rate. She looked at me quizzically and asked how long I would stay. Well, eight years later, I checked out of the hotel! And what an adventure it was along the way.

—Joe Sigelman, founder, OfficeTiger
(now owned by RR Donnelley)

The India that extended their perimeters of vision was less a geographical place and more an internal transformation—a voyage outward and inward simultaneously.

—Jeffery Paine, *Father India: How Encounters with an Ancient Culture Transformed the Modern West*

If you are going to stay in India for more than six months, you are required to register with Foreigners Registration Office, or the local police station if your city does not have such an office. If you are going to work in India, you must have an employment visa. India generally taxes worldwide personal income (as does the United States), so it's a good idea to consult a tax specialist in your home country as well as in India for tax planning. Even if you don't intend to drive regularly in India, it is also a good idea to obtain an international driver's license from your home state's department of motor vehicles or equivalent authority; in some areas of the United States, the AAA can issue international permits.

If you are establishing your company's India operation, or if you are a top executive, your company might start you on an expatriate package, which may include a Western salary plus benefits for travel, accommodation, schooling for your children, et cetera. These expatriate premium benefits sometimes fade away for long-term residents or for companies that exceed a certain head count. Some multinational companies with a large footprint in India not only take away expatriate premiums, but start to offer only salaries at Indian market levels; at lower and middle levels, such compensation may not be attractive to Westerners.

In recent years, young Americans have begun to take internships and even entry-level jobs at fast-growing companies in India simply to gain the international experience. Certain industries, such as aviation, telecommunications, and oil exploration, attract a number of expatriates at higher levels. For example, many commercial pilots in India are expatriates, as are the CEOs of several airlines based in India. Tata Sons board member R. Gopalakrishnan told me, "We presently have a few non-Indians running some of our companies today; for example the CEO of Taj Hotels is an American, Raymond Bickson. The former CEO of Tata Teleservices Darryl Green is an American, and the CEO of Tata Technologies is American, Pat McGoldrick." Broadly speaking, however, India is not yet an attractive relocation destination for top employees from the West. This section will clear up some misconceptions.

Former General Electric executive Scott Bayman's advice is to "get local fast." He recommends that you engage with Indian industry and with Indian society as quickly as possible upon your arrival. "Don't just hang out with other expatriates. Make an effort to meet Indians and get to understand how things work there. Too many times expatriates tend to get together with other expatriates to have these discussions about how difficult things are and the problems of living and doing business in India."

Mason Byles chose to stay in an area where all his neighbors were Indian. He saw a very different India by visiting people's homes, being invited for weddings, having dinner with them, meeting their children, and getting a glimpse into their lives.

India is family-friendly. The American embassy runs excellent schools in several major cities. Several expatriates told me that their India postings brought their families

closer together and that their children received a better
K–12 education than they might have back in the United
States. "New Delhi has the best American school you could
find. My daughters, Patricia and Amanda, who went to the
school, have both done very well in college," John Triplett
shares. "Patricia went on to Bowdoin and the University of
Connecticut; Amanda is at Sarah Lawrence."

A top executive confided that expatriate wives prefer
India to some other Asian postings, because "you won't
find young women in India who want to separate the man
from his wife in order to secure American residency." Some
single men are disappointed in India because it does not
offer the vibrant nightlife of Bangkok, Hong Kong, or other
foreign locations. Single women will not find themselves
lacking for attention in most Indian cities.

If you are married or in a relationship, you should be
aware that your partner or spouse will likely have a much
harder time adjusting to India than you will. Many expatriate postings to India fail because the spouse has difficulty
with the change. Jobs for spouses are few and don't pay
well, and the pressures and excitement of work will engage you fully upon arrival. After the initial euphoria, your
spouse will have long periods during days (and weeks if
you travel within India) where he or she could be idle,
bored, or worse. It is very important to have open and
ongoing communication on how to make the experience
in India productive for the spouse. Some larger companies
actually provide professional help in this regard.

School-aged children who must move to India also need

time to prepare and adjust to the shock. They need to maintain connectivity by e-mail and instant messaging to old friends, but should also understand that they must reach out to their classmates and neighbors in their new location. In some ways, the children of today have an easier time since Western video games, pop music, and text messaging are equally appealing to youth worldwide, at least to those whose parents can afford these amenities. Children have a harder time understanding class and economic barriers in India. Academic standards and homework expectations at Indian schools may put your children and you under some stress.

Most expatriates who live in houses or apartments in India will have extensive household help. A chauffeur to take them to work. Another chauffeur for the family and for weekends. A cook and/or housekeeper. A nanny if you have young children. A watchman or two if you are in a bungalow. Laundry, housecleaning, grocery shopping, washing the car, mowing the grass (if you are lucky enough to have grass) are all taken care of by hired help. Anything you buy can be home-delivered on demand— from one egg or one rented DVD to a sofa, television, or car. It's the good life, in many ways, and it is hard to give up when you return to your original country.

Finding a Home

Commute times in Indian cities, particularly at peak hours, can be unbearable. While most Indians work on their laptop computers or cell phones during the drive to and from work, your individual comfort with spending time on the roads will define the outer boundaries within which you wish to stay. Apartments and homes offered primarily to foreigners are usually premium-priced and may offer slightly higher levels of service. In major cities, you may also find a few "serviced apartments" and similar long-term-stay alternatives, but for the most part finding a home in India can be a bit of an adventure. Third parties do exist to assist in the search, but you may find it productive to supplement their efforts with your own. The trend toward high-rise condominiums began in Mumbai decades ago, but today most cities have such alternatives. Single-family detached homes are much more expensive (and almost unavailable in Mumbai). You may also be offered "duplexes," usually two-story town houses. Many landlords require a deposit of as much as ten months' rent and a lease of eleven or twelve months.

Ask about backup electric power offered by the landlord, which may be provided by a large battery, "inverter," or central generator but may only power your refrigerator and a few lights. Most expatriates should inquire about placing a backup generator to power the air-conditioning during the frequent utility outages. Also ask about the source of water, and don't be surprised if a multifamily unit has its own "tubewell" on the premises; municipal supply can be limited in some cities. You will want to install a reverse-osmosis (RO) system for drinking water. Locally provided RO systems are packaged with service agreements and can provide you bug-free water. Piped natural gas (PNG) for cooking is starting to be offered in some cities, but most urban homes depend on red cylinders of liquefied petroleum gas (LPG) for cooking. Kitchens are generally smaller than in the West and may not have a place for a Western-style range and oven. In some cases, your refrigerator and microwave may need to sit in the dining area.

Ensure that bathrooms meet your expectations, especially if you are looking on your own. Some older homes may only offer Indian-style squatting toilets. Many Indians consider the use of toilet paper to be unhygienic, and most Western toilets in India now include a bidet-type attachment. Western-style bathtubs are a rarity; *taking a bath* means taking a shower. In some cases, hot water from the wall-mounted "geyser" only feeds the faucet under the shower, while sinks and showers run cold water. Due to unreliable electric power, don't be surprised if your bathroom has a gas cylinder sitting on the floor that powers a gas-fired wall-mounted water heater. Water in the bathroom may be supplied from a large storage tank on the roof, which may not be completely sealed. Never, never drink that water unless you have boiled it. If you do have a municipal water supply, ask if you will get twenty-four-hour running water and how often the supply may fail.

Wood-and-drywall construction is rare in India. Most floors are hard terrazzo or marble; most walls are brick or concrete. Multiunit buildings generally have small, tight parking spots in the "basement," which may sometimes be at ground level. The "first floor" in India is actually the second floor; they start counting with the "ground floor."

Zoning is not enforced in most Indian cities, and you will find banks, shops, and other commercial establishments occupying structures that were clearly meant only for residential use. The lower floors of high-rise condos are also attractive to all manner of small businesses in some cities, from computer tutors to beauty parlors and physicians who may run a part-time practice from their homes. Your neighbors may be busier, noisier, and nosier than you expect in the West. Be gracious to the nosy neighbors; you will need their help soon.

Settling In

It will take you longer to settle in your new home in India than the equivalent experience in the West. So don't vacate your hotel room until you have electric power, backup power, gas, water, drinking water, and working appliances in place.

You can receive a multitude of TV channels including CNN, MTV India, Discovery, and BBC via your neighborhood cable provider, who is likely to be a small local entrepreneur with a crew that slings those cobwebs of wire dangling from many residential buildings. Direct-to-home satellite broadcasting with small antennas is now offered in India. Mark Bullard found that he missed live sporting events, so he installed Slingbox, which enables him to watch live TV from his home in the United States over the Internet.

Ordering telephone service is much simpler than it used to be. In most cities, broadband Internet service is also offered by several telephone providers. In newer construction, you may find yourself ahead of offerings in the West, with an ultra-high-speed fiber-optic cable terminating in your building. While many Indians get by with a cell phone only, I recommend that you have at least one wired phone line in your home. In the case of a local disaster, the government may temporarily shut off cell service, and you may find that the Internet and landline service turn out to be good alternative channels of communication.

You will also need to determine what household help you want to hire, and then locate such staff. It is best to use local expertise. The English-speaking skills of such staff are highly variable, and you may pay a stiff premium if that is a requirement. Language is not an issue unique to expatriates. I spent a year living in south India where our cook spoke only Tamil; my apartment mate and I depended on sign language for most communications, supplemented by occasional guidance from our landlady, who spoke four Indian languages in addition to English.

Conclusion

Mason Byles, who is now retired from Hewlett-Packard, reminisces, "India is a beautiful, diverse, exciting, sometimes chaotic, sometimes peaceful, wonderful country. I miss it all every day I am away."

If you are timid, you can make a weeklong trip to India, never stir out of your plush hotel or company conference room, and go back wondering what all the fuss in this chapter was about. There are also those expatriates who spend a year or two in India and try to interact only with their own compatriots or perhaps other expatriates. Indians don't trust them and seldom develop much regard for them. They are usually ineffective in bringing profits to their companies, but, even worse, they poison the atmosphere for those who may succeed them. With the simple guidelines in this chapter, you can travel to India and even live there while being quite productive for your business and your company.

CONCLUSION

The Song Behind the Words

The voices around me spoke in all the dialects of India, and not for the first time, I was struck by the notion that I was just one alien among many. This seemed to be a nation of millions of foreigners, a bewildering accretion of mutually exclusive tongues, gods, and cultures the governance of which, shaky although it might be, appeared nothing short of miraculous.
    —Alexander Frater, *Chasing the Monsoon*, 1986

As I left the village for the last time, . . . I had the feeling that I had just begun. It was as if I had peeled off one and a half layers of fifty, and what I had learned was only an early glimmering of truth.
    —Elisabeth Bumiller, *May You Be the Mother of a Hundred Sons*, 1990

If you read books like I do and have reached the concluding chapter by skipping certain sections, let me redirect you specifically to chapter 2, "India in Context." Read or reread that chapter if you want to appreciate the reasons underlying some of the paradoxes that you might encounter when you do business in India.

Western companies today, regardless of industry or size, have unprecedented opportunity to profit from a relationship with India. I travel to India frequently, often with my clients. The boundless energy and enthusiasm of Indian executives and entrepreneurs is infectious. While there may be short-term setbacks, the trend for India's globalization over the next couple of decades is doubtless going to be positive. For Western companies, it is my view that this rising tide will not lift all boats. Some companies will fail; and a few will fail dramatically. I hope that, having read this book, you have reduced your risk of becoming like one of the blind men that I described in the introduction.

R. Gopalakrishnan, executive director of Tata Sons and former vice chairman of Unilever's operation in India, put it very succinctly: "The day that you think you have understood India, stop and unlearn. India is complex, and if you are new to it, you can get that false feeling that you have actually understood far too soon. Then, when India does not behave as you expect, you start thinking of Indians as unreliable or difficult. You must learn to listen to the song behind the words."

Appreciating this song requires very careful listening and cross-cultural skills. Often it requires patience, persistence, and an open mind. It requires the ability to deal with ambiguity. Sometimes it requires the guidance of an expert. Very often it requires all of the above. This book has provided you the basic vocabulary to begin to understand. But to profit from India, you must engage. And when you engage with India, be it for a day or a decade, it can and will transform you. In the twenty-first century, it can transform your company's bottom line and make you a hero. And in some cases it may continue to draw you back after retirement.

India is an elephant. Enjoy the ride.

ACKNOWLEDGMENTS

I absolutely love helping Western companies deal with India, and Amritt's clients make it possible for my colleagues and me to make a living. Many of the insights in this book are derived and validated from client assignments, and I am deeply grateful for that experience.

Equally, I am indebted to the executive attendees of the seminar on "Business with India." As co-instructor and now as instructor for the seminar, I have learned as much from the attendees over the years as they have from me. Their questions and comments invigorate my teaching and provide me incentive to keep the material fresh. I am grateful to Nick Nichols, director of the California Institute of Technology's Industrial Relations Center (IRC), for the vision to initiate this seminar, to my former co-instructor David

Everhart for teaching it with me several times, and to the entire staff of the IRC.

While I chose to write the book, my wife, Smita, was involuntarily drafted into the role of sanity checker, pre-editor, researcher, and more. My children, Avi and Anshika, also sacrificed numerous evenings and weekends and part of their summer as I delved into a project that became bigger than I had imagined. I am lucky to have such a responsive and understanding family.

In writing this book, I made a deliberate decision to reach beyond Amritt clients to offer a wide but pragmatic perspective on doing business in India. I was humbled and awed by those who made time to help me in this effort.

In alphabetical order by first name, I want to thank Ajit Nazre, Alok Agarwal, Alok Sethi, Anil Kapur, Ann Winblad, Anshika Bagla, Arjun Malhotra, Ashank Desai, Avi Bagla, Dr. Avinash Agrawal, Baba Kalyani, Bala Vasireddi, Bhavesh Muni, Dr. Bill Overholt, Bob Nichols, Brendan Weier, Carmine D'Alisio, Dr. Christopher Flores, C. S. Suryanarayanan, David Bradley, Dominic Price, Don Hollis, Gary McAvoy, Geeta Goel, Dr. Guy Rabbat, Dr. Hema Bagla, John Triplett, Joseph Sigelman, K. V. Kamath, Kapil Bagla, Karun Varma, Kashi Memani, Kevin Bonfield, Kinjal Medh, Lonnie Sapp, Kristin Paulson, Lalit Jalan, M. L. Cessna, M. G. Parameswaran, Mark Bullard, Mark J. Riedy, Mason Byles, Michael Ducker, Michael Freund, Muktesh Pant, Nirmal Goel, Pallava Bagla, Parveen Gulati, Pinaki Ghosh, Dr. Pawan Kumar Goenka, Pradeep Gupta, R. Gopalakrishnan, Rajesh Dalal, Rajesh

Kumar, Rajesh Subramaniam, Rakesh Pandey, Robyn Meredith, Ron Somers, Sameer Chandra, Sandeep Chaudhary, Dr. Sandeep Muju, Sanjay Nayar, Saurabh Goel, Scott Bayman, Shan Nair, Shantanu Surpure, Dr. Sharad Bagla, Shesh Kulkarni, Smita Bagla, Dr. Stanley Wolpert, Stuart Creighton, Dr. Subhadra Menon, Subodh Bhargava, Sukanya Ghosh, Suketu Mehta, Sukhjinder Bhatti, Syed Athar Abbas, Dr. Tim Lenihan, Dr. Uday Karmarkar, Dr. Vasant Joshi, Vinay Agarwal, Vince Thompson, Vinod Dham, Vishal Gandhi, Vishwavir Ahuja, and Vivek Kudva.

My editor at Hachette Book Group USA, Leila Porteous, and her colleagues, including at least Jamie Raab, Kallie Shimek, Laura Jorstad, Peggy Boelke, and Robert Nissen, plus many others whom I never met, have ensured the book is readable and timely, and has made it into your hands. My thanks to them all.

The first author I ever met was my father, Dr. Sitaram Bagla, who passed away in 1995. His determination and humility continue to inspire me to this day.

GLOSSARY OF INDIAN ENGLISH

For the most up-to-date version of this glossary you can visit www.amritt.com/IndianEnglish.html.

Abey! Hey you!

Achchaa! Okay (from Hindi)

Aeroplane Airplane

Alloh Hello (when answering the phone)

Almirah Cupboard, cabinet, sometimes closet; also called almari

Alms Money or in-kind charity, to beggars or to organizations; the word is archaic in America, common in India

Alright Okay

Amma   In north India, mother; in south India, female (kid or adult)

Annexure   Appendix ("Please look at Annexure B of our report for financials")

Ans.   Answer (abbreviation)

At the rate of   @, at (for e-mail addresses: "My e-mail is jay at the rate of aol.com")

Auto   Auto-rickshaw; a three-wheeler open taxi, also called a tuk-tuk in Southeast Asia

Averagely   On average

Baap re!   Exclamation of surprise, literally "Oh daddy!"

Babu   Bureaucrat, clerk, sometimes boss

Babu English   Pejorative for grammatically incorrect English written by a fellow Indian

Back   Ago ("We met three days back")

Badmash   See *hooligan*

Balti   Bucket; also a type of cuisine ("balti chicken")

Bandh   General strike in which commercial establishments may be shut down

Bapu   Literally "father," the term often refers to Mahatma Gandhi, the "Father of India"

Basement   Usually, underground parking in a condo; basements as living space are rare

Batchmate   Classmate

Bearer   (1) Waiter (in a restaurant); (2) cash (on a cheque or financial document)

Bhai/bhaiya   Man, dude; literally, "brother"

Black money   Money that is untaxed and undocumented

to the government; also called black; see also *white money*

Board   Signboard or sign; see also *hoarding*

Bogey   Coach (in a passenger train)

Bonnet   Hood (of an automobile)

Boot   Trunk (of an automobile)

Bowled   Knocked out (from cricket)

Brinjal   Eggplant

Britisher   Briton

Broking   Brokerage

Brother   May be a brother or cousin; see *real brother*

Bungalow   Any big house, typically with a veranda, driveway, and walled front yard

Bunk   (verb) To avoid classes in school

Bus!   Enough! That's it (from Hindi)

By   The symbol referred to as a slash; divided by; "two by three" means two-thirds

CA   Chartered Accountant, similar to a Certified Public Accountant

Cabin   Office, cubicle

Calling card   Business card; see also *visiting card*

Cantt   Cantonment; the area in a city reserved for military installations and housing

Car park   Parking lot

Cash memo   Invoice, receipt (in a retail store)

Cent percent   100 percent

Chaat   Spicy fresh snack food

Challo!   Let's go!

Chamcha   Sycophant, a person who is a suck-up; literally, a large spoon or ladle

Chappals   Slippers

Chaprasi   Messenger

Chawl   Tenement; see also *kholi*

Chemist   Pharmacist; see also *druggist*

Chennai   The new name for Madras, a major southern city and the capital of Tamil Nadu state

Cheque   Check (as in a bank check)

Chowk   Urban square, market, major intersection

Christian name   First name; see also *forename* and *surname*

Ciggy   Cigarette (slang)

Cinema   Movie, or movie theater

Cinema hall   Movie theater

Co-brother   For a married man, his wife's sister's husband; used most often in south India

Cold drink   Beverage (Coke, milk shake, lemonade)

Colony   Neighborhood or American subdivision ("I grew up in Nehru Colony")

Come again   Please repeat what you said, I did not understand you the first time

Con call   Conference phone call, usually at a prearranged time

Convent school   A school run by Christian missionaries, often nuns; loosely, any Christian school

Corporate   Company ("The top three corporates in town are our customers")

Cousin brother   Cousin, male

Cousin sister Cousin, female

Cowdung Cow chips, used as fertilizer and as fuel for village fires

Crockery Chinaware; fragile dishes

Crore Ten million; see also *lakh*

CTC Cost to Company (when referring to the total compensation of an employee, including benefits)

Cupboard Cabinet

Dal Lentils; also the dish cooked with lentils and a major protein source in Indian diets; also called dhall

Degree holder Someone who has a bachelor's degree (diploma) from the equivalent of a four-year college; considered more qualified than a *diploma holder*

Dekho, dekko To take a look, to examine, to watch out of curiosity (from Hindi)

Departmental store Any self-service shop, even a small one

Desi Fellow countryman; used by Indians abroad to refer to one another

Dickey, dicky Trunk (of an automobile)

Diploma holder One who has completed a two- or three-year college course, such as in an American junior college; considered less qualified than a *degree holder*

District County, in local government

DM District Magistrate; the seniormost local government official at the county level; often an officer of the Indian Administrative Service

Donkey's years A long time

Dosa   South Indian crêpe, often filled with potatoes, eaten as a snack

Double-roti   Sandwich bread

Dress   Outfit, clothing (for men or women)

Driver   Chauffeur

Druggist   Pharmacist; see also *chemist*

Duplex   Two-level house (*not* two houses with a common wall); often pronounced *duplay*

Eggetarian   A vegetarian who also eats eggs and egg products

E-mail ID   E-mail address ("Please give me your e-mail ID")

EMI   Equated monthly installments; a level-payment plan to repay capital or revolving loans

Engaged   Busy (for a telephone line: "I gave you a tinkle but your number was engaged")

Fag   Cigarette (slang; the word is not used as a slur for a homosexual)

Fagged out   Tired, exhausted

Farm   For a wealthy urban resident, a cottage or resort in the country with little or no agriculture

FD   Fixed deposit, same as a CD or certificate of deposit at a US bank

Filter coffee   Brewed coffee, as opposed to instant

Firangi   Foreigner

Fired   Chastised (*not* removed from a job: "Every time Jay misses a meeting, the boss fires him for tardiness")

First floor   Second story of a multistory building; see *ground floor*

Flat   Apartment

Fly.   "And family members"; often seen on group tickets ("Mr. Singh, Mrs. Singh, and 2 fly.")

Football   Soccer; American football is not played in India

Footfalls   The number of prospective and real customers to enter the store (in a retail business)

Footpath   Sidewalk

Foreign returned   Having recently come back from some foreign country

Forename   First name; see also *Christian name*

Franked   The act of applying metered postage, using a *franking machine*

Franking machine   Postage meter

Freak out   Let's have fun (slang)

French beard   A goatee

Fresher   Freshman; first-year student, new employee, inexperienced worker

Full stop   Period, at the end of a sentence

Ghee   Clarified butter, often used as a cooking medium

Godman   Pejorative word for a person who claims to have supernatural powers

Godown   Warehouse

Godrej   Steel *almirah;* after the brand name of a leading India company

Goggles   Sunglasses; also called swimming goggles

Good name   Name ("I am Jay, what is your good name, please?")

Gratuity   Payment for meritorious service; not the same as a tip

Ground floor   First floor (American-style) of a multistory building; see *first floor*

Guru   Respected and revered teacher

Haina   Isn't it? (used as a confirmatory filler at the end of a sentence)

Hai Ram   Oh God!—an exclamation of surprise, frustration, excitement ("Hai Ram, I can't believe I got the job!")

Half-pants   Shorts, knickerbockers; also called nekar

Half-ticket   Reduced-price ticket for a child, senior, or other special category

Handle   Handlebar of a bicycle, steering wheel of a car

Hash   #: that is, the pound symbol

Hat trick   Three in a row (from cricket)

Have   Exhortation to eat/drink something offered to a guest

Healthy   In north India, refers to fat people, but not pejoratively

Hero   In a movie, leading man or male star

Heroine   In a movie, leading woman

High Court   The highest court in the state; each state in India has a High Court (see *Supreme Court*)

History sheeter   Person with a long history of violations or crimes

Hoarding   Billboard

Hockey   Field hockey, played on grass with a ball and wooden hockey sticks; *not* ice hockey, which is virtually unknown in India

Homely   One who can build a good home, has upstanding moral values (most often referring to a marriage-able young woman)

Hooligan Hoodlum, unruly person

Hotel Eating establishment, restaurant

IAS Indian Administrative Service; the elite civil service cadre that runs the country

Iddly In south India, a steamed rice or lentil patty, traditionally eaten at breakfast

Indent (noun) Purchase order; official requisition for goods or services

Indian-Made Foreign Liquor Whiskey, rum, gin, or the like produced in India—but not "country liquor," which is usually much less expensive and sold in different stores; also called IMFL

Intimate you Inform you

Into Multiplied by ("Two into three is six")

Invigilator Monitor (as in an administered test or examination)

Item girl It girl; a female movie star who appears in an "item song" in a Hindi movie; "the talk of the town"

Jai Hail (salutation), such as Jai Ganesh (to a god) or Jai Hind (to the country)

Jawan Soldier; the equivalent of a US private

Ji (suffix) Used to refer to anyone meriting respect (Parker-ji, Smith-ji, Gupta-ji)

Jija-ji Sister's husband (as a pronoun or a suffix: "Ramesh Jija-ji will be over for dinner")

Jugaad Creative improvisation, jury-rigging; to find a way out by hook or by crook

Keep (1) To put; (2) mistress (pejorative: "a kept woman")

Kem cho? How are you? (in Gujarati, a language spoken in the western state of Gujarat and in Mumbai)

Kholi In Mumbai, tenement; see also *chawl*

Kitty party A gathering of housewives, often accompanied by potluck meals, or lately by network marketing

Kolkata The new name for Calcutta, a large city in east India and the capital of West Bengal state

Kyoon? Why? (from Hindi)

Laat-sahib The big boss (from Lord Sahib—the governor general or viceroy in colonial India)

Lacuna Gap, shortcoming, failing

Ladyfinger Okra, a vegetable

Lakh Hundred thousand, written as 1,00,000; also called lac; see *crore*

Lift (1) Elevator; (2) to ride ("Can you please give me a lift to the airport? The bus is running late")

Load shedding Brownouts or blackouts, often prescheduled, due to electric power shortages

Local Suburban train (in Mumbai)

Lorry Truck

Love marriage A marriage that follows a love affair, as opposed to a more common "arranged marriage," which is arranged by the bride's and groom's parents

Madam Respectful term for woman—same as ma'am ("Don't worry, madam, the taxi will be waiting for you at 6:00 AM.")

Maggu   Bookish person, one who studies a lot, someone who memorizes answers

Mahatma Gandhi   Mohandas Karamchand Gandhi, freedom fighter, revered as the Father of Independent India

Mall Road   Main Street; the English colonialists often named the major street Mall Road; most Mall Roads have been renamed to Mahatma Gandhi Road or MG Road

Mama   Maternal uncle; also street talk for "cop"

Marks   Points ("He received 92 percent marks on the exam")

Matter   Material, content ("Please give me the matter for your Web site")

MBBS   Bachelor of medicine and bachelor of surgery (a physician)

MD   Managing director, equivalent of a CEO ("My MD must approve any discounts on shipping cost")

Meat   Any food of animal origin (chicken, pork, lamb, fish, et cetera)

Medium wave radio   AM radio

Memsaab   Honorific to refer to a woman boss or woman of higher status (from *ma'am sahib*)

Messrs.   For a corporation ("Messrs. Procter & Gamble")

Military hotel   A restaurant that serves nonvegetarian food; the term is most often used in Tamil Nadu state, where many are vegetarian

Miscreants   People up to no good; petty criminals

Missed call   A call that is deliberately unanswered on a cell phone, as a signal ("Give me a missed call when you are ready for me to pick you up")

Missi amma   In Karnataka, often used to refer to an Anglo-Indian or Christian woman, one who may wear a skirt

Mixie   Grinder, blender

Mobile   Cell phone

Modalities   Processes, paperwork (bureaucratese)

Mother tongue   Native language

Mufti   Off-duty clothes of someone who wears a uniform at work (from the British Indian army)

Mumbai   The new name for Bombay, the capital of Maharashtra state and also the most populous Indian city

My Mrs.   My wife

Namaste   A greeting; literally, "I respect you"

Near and dear   Friends and family

Nearly   Can mean "approximately" rather than "almost" ("We have nearly ten to twelve vice presidents")

Needful   Whatever needs to be done ("I will do the needful")

Nekar   Shorts, knickerbockers; also called nikkar

NGO   Nongovernmental organization, usually in reference to private nonprofit groups

Note   Bill of currency ("I will give you a hundred-rupee note")

NRI   Nonresident Indian; an Indian citizen residing overseas

Numbers   Each (as a measure of quantity: "Please send me three numbers of ingots" means "Please send me three ingots")

Nursing home Small private hospital, usually owned by a physician; *not* a retirement home

Oblique The symbol referred to as a slash; "My address is Seven Oblique A" refers to 7/A; also see *by*

Obsequies Funeral rites

Offs Holiday or vacation day ("days that I am off")

Oof! An interjection implying distress or frustration; ugh

Out of station Out of town ("Sorry I could not meet you, I was out of station when you visited")

Parallely In parallel

Party Entity, company ("I want to you to meet a promising party who may place a large order")

Passed out Graduated (from college)

Passout To graduate, to complete an education ("I am a 1996 passout from Delhi University")

Pavement Sidewalk; *not* the street

Pay-in slip Deposit slip (at a bank)

Pen-down strike A strike or protest in which office workers sit at their desks but do no work

Peon Unskilled office helper

Pet name Nickname ("My brother is Krishna, but we gave him the pet name *Kris*")

Petrol Gasoline

Petrol pump Gas station

PFA Please find attached (an abbreviation often used as part of an e-mail)

PIN code Six-digit Postal Code (*PIN* stands for "Postal Index Number"), the equivalent of a zip code

Pin-drop silence   Absolute silence, where you might hear the sound of a pin drop

Plinth   Built-up area (in real estate)

Postgraduate   Graduate; a student pursuing education beyond a bachelor's degree

Postman   Mailman

Prepone   To move an event to an earlier date or time (as opposed to postpone)

PTO   Please turn over (an annotation at the bottom of a page to indicate further content)

Public school   A prestigious (and very private) school; similar to British public schools

Pucca, pukka   Solid, real, the real thing; literally, "ripe"

Puncher   Puncture

Puncture   Flat (on an automobile tire)

Pune   The new name for Poona, near Mumbai

Purse   Purse or wallet for a man or woman

Puts in papers   Announces the decision to resign ("Jay Aman put in his papers last week")

Pyjama   Loose pants worn by men in north India, not just for sleeping

Q   Line; also spelled queue ("Please form a Q in front of the ticket counter")

Ragging   Hazing or harassment of new students by seniors

Raise an invoice   Create an invoice

Rapeseed   Canola seed for oil

Ration card   A government-issued document that entitles the holder to price-controlled food; also serves as an ID

Real brother   Brother, as distinct from a cousin or *cousin brother*

Regularise   Legitimize

Retiring room   Waiting room for travelers at a railway or bus station; a retiring room may include a sleeping area

Revert   Get back to you (by phone or e-mail: "Give me a week to revert to you")

Rick   Rickshaw (slang)

Ring   Phone call ("Give me a ring tomorrow")

Roti   Bread; see also *double-roti*

Rubber   Eraser (*not* condom)

Sahib   Boss, often used to refer to a person of higher status; also called sa'ab; see also *memsahib*

Samosa   A triangular fried snack food filled with potatoes, perhaps meat; similar to an empanada

Scheme   Plan, project (no negative connotation)

Scooter   Sometimes used in north India to refer to a scooter-rickshaw taxi; see also *auto*

Seniors   More experienced employees or students; *not* older people

Sexy   Extremely cool, slick

Shop   Retail store

Shri   Mister, Mr.; also called Shree or Sri

Shrimati   Mrs.; also called Srimati or Sreemati

Sir   Used in place of a person's name as an honorific; see *ji* ("Sanjay Sir authorized me to buy this computer")

Sit   To have an office ("I sit in London and Delhi")

Sixer   Home run (slang, from cricket)

Sleeper   Cross-tie; the cross-member that connects rail-road tracks

SMS   Text messaging

Smt.   *Shrimati*, Mrs.; also called Srimati or Sreemati

Speak in English   Speak English

Specs   Spectacles, glasses

Speed-breaker   Road bump

Stamp paper   A government-issued paper for the signing of legal documents, as a tax collection method

Stand   (1) Trade show booth, kiosk; (2) to run for elective office

Standard   School year or grade ("My son is in sixth standard")

Stay   To live ("Where do you stay in Chicago?")

STD   Long-distance phone call (*STD* stands for "Subscriber Trunk Dialing")

Steel frame   Indian Administrative Service, IAS: the steel frame that holds up the Indian edifice

Stepney   Spare tire (in an automobile); sometimes used insultingly to refer to a mistress (spare wife)

Stockist   A dealer or retailer who maintains inventory of a particular item

Studio   Photo studio

Supreme Court   The highest court in India; there is only one Supreme Court, not one per state; see *High Court*

Surname   Last name; see also *forename* and *Christian name*

Take   To consume (when used with food or drink items: "Take a cold drink, please")

Tap   Faucet

Tea   Hot tea, often served with milk and sugar premixed unless you specify in advance

Tehsil   An official administrative subdivision of a county or district

Telecon   Telephone conference, or business telephone call

Thali   Dinner plate, often made of stainless steel

Thali meal   A fixed-price all-you-can-eat meal, usually at a midpriced restaurant

Tharra   Country liquor, as distinct from IMFL; tharra is often a drink of the lower socioeconomic classes

Throw up   Bring up, cause to happen (*not* vomit)

Tick   Check off (*not* irritate: "Please tick the preferred time for your appointment on this list")

Tie-up   Joint venture; agreement to work together

Tiffin   Meal, especially a short meal or one that you carry with you

Tiffin carrier   Lunchbox, lunch pail

Timepass   (1) Wasting time; (2) snack food such as peanuts, sold on buses, on trains, and in stations

Tinkle   Phone call ("Give me a tinkle next time you are in town and we can meet")

Toilet   Restroom; see also *WC*

Too good   Very good ("Your presentation today was too good")

Torch   Flashlight

Tubelight   Fluorescent light

Turnover   Revenue

Tyre   Automobile tire

Under root   Square root (in mathematics)

Updation   Updating

Upgradation   Process of applying an upgrade

Upto   Up to

Use and throw   Disposable

Vakalat-naama   Affidavit

Vanaspati   Of vegetable or vegetarian origin ("vanaspati oil")

Vernac   Provincial; culturally backward or unrefined (from *vernacular*)

Vide   Refer to ("You owe us $32,570 vide Invoice Number 3275/F")

Visiting card   Business card; see also *calling card*

Wallah   Person employed in a certain capacity or connected to a certain activity ("The taxi-wallah knew Kolkata very well")

WC   Water closet, toilet

White goods   Major appliances (in retailing; *not* linens)

White money   Money that is shown on the books and duly taxed; also white; see also *black money*

Windscreen   Windshield (of an automobile)

Wine   This can refer to alcoholic liquor; you may not find any Chablis at a wine shop!

Works   (noun) Factory, plant

Yaar   Friend, amigo, buddy (slang, Hindi); also called yar

Yallow   Hello (when answering the phone)

Yesterday night   Last night

Your good name please?   What is your name?

Zed   Zee (the last letter of the alphabet)

BIBLIOGRAPHY

Introduction

Ahya, Chetan, Andy Xie, Stephen Roach, Mihir Sheth, and Denise Yam. *India and China: The New Tigers of Asia. Part II, Special Economic Analysis.* Mumbai: Morgan Stanley Research, 2006.

Aillawadi, Yogesh, "Planet Mars: Mukesh v. Anil," http://astrospeak.indiatimes.com/articleshow/978971.cms (last accessed December 8, 2007).

"Elephant Empathy," *Economist,* July 27, 2006, http://www.economist.com/science/displaystory.cfm?story_id=E1_SNTRQTT (last accessed December 8, 2007).

"Elephants Mourn Their Dead," November 4, 2005, http://www.abc.net.au/science/news/stories/s1497634.htm (last accessed December 8, 2007).

"Hungry Tiger, Dancing Elephant," *Economist,* April 4, 2007, http://www.economist.com/printedition/display

Story.cfm?Story_ID=8956676 (last accessed December 8, 2007).

"India: Why Apple Walked Away," *BusinessWeek,* June 19, 2006, http://www.businessweek.com/magazine/content/06_25/b3989058.htm (last accessed December 8, 2007).

Kripalani, Manjeet, "IBM's Pep Rally," *BusinessWeek,* June 6, 2006,http://www.businessweek.com/globalbiz/content/jun2006/gb20060606_283521.htm (last accessed December 8, 2007).

"NASSCOM Announces Top 20 IT Software and Service Exporters in India," June 16, 2005 (apparently modified at IBM's request), http://www.nasscom.in/Nasscom/templates/NormalPage.aspx?id=2717 (last accessed December 8, 2007).

"Starbucks: A Passage to India," *CNN Money,* November 1, 2004,http://money.cnn.com/2004/10/28/news/fortune500/starbucks_india/index.htm (last accessed May 31, 2007).

"Starbucks Puts India Plan on Hold," *USA Today,* July 25, 2007,http://www.usatoday.com/news/topstories/2007-07-25-3427986509_x.htm.

Wilson, Dominic, and Roopa Purushothaman. *Dreaming with BRICS: The Path to 2050. A Goldman Sachs Research Report. Global Economics Paper Number 99.* http://www2.goldmansachs.com/insight/research/reports/99.pdf (last accessed December 8, 2007).

Chapter 1: The Big Opportunities

Apte, U., U. Karmarkar, and H. Nath, "Information Services in the US Economy: Value, Jobs and Management Implications," UCLA BIT Project Working Paper (2007).

Chapter 2: India in Context

Allen, Charles, ed. *Plain Tales from the Raj.* London: Futura Publications, 1976.

The CIA World Fact Book. https://www.cia.gov/library/publications/the-world-factbook/geos/in.html#Econ (last accessed February 12, 2008).

Hijiya, James A., "The Gita of Robert Oppenheimer," http://www.aps-pub.com/proceedings/1442/Hijiya.pdf (last accessed December 8, 2007).

Indian Aid for Katrina: Press Release, http://www.indianembassy.org/press_release/2005/Sept/11.htm (last accessed December 8, 2007).

Kumar, Arun. *The Black Economy in India.* New Delhi: Penguin Books India, 2002.

Maddison, Angus. *The World Economy: A Millennial Perspective (OECD Development Centre Studies).* Paris: OECD Development Centre, 2001.

Mehta, Suketu. *Maximum City: Bombay Lost and Found.* New York: Vintage Books, 2004.

Robins, Nick. *The Corporation That Changed the World: How the East India Company Shaped the Modern Multinational.* London: Pluto Press, 2006.

Tripathi, Dwijendra, and Jyoti Jumani. *The Concise Oxford History of Indian Business.* New Delhi: Oxford University Press, 2007.

Wolpert, Stanley. *A New History of India.* New York: Oxford University Press, 2000.

Chapter 3: Cross-Cultural Communication

Bennet, Milton J., ed. *Basic Concepts of Intercultural Communications: Selected Readings.* London: Intercultural Press, 2000.

Culture Matters, *The Peace Corps Cross-Cultural Workbook.* Washington, DC: US Government Printing Office, no date.

India: World's Second Largest English Speaking Country. Teachers of English to Speakers of Other Languages in India Web site. http://tesol-india.ac.in/EnglishTeaching Industry/en/india-worlds-second-largest-english -speaking-country (last accessed December 7, 2007).

Kumar, R. "Brahmanical Idealism, Anarchical Individualism, and the Dynamics of Indian Negotiating Behavior," *International Journal of Cross-Cultural Management* 4 (2004): 39–58.

Levine, Robert. *A Geography of Time: The Temporal Misadventures of a Social Psychologist, or How Every Culture Keeps Time Just a Little Bit Differently.* New York: Basic Books Publishing, 1997.

Power, Carla, "Not the Queen's English," *Newsweek,* International Edition, March 7, 2007, http://www.msnbc

.msn.com/id/7038031/site/newsweek (last accessed May 31, 2007).

Salacuse, Jeswald. *The Global Negotiator.* New York: Palgrave Macmillan, 2003.

Sen, Amartya. *The Argumentative Indian: Writings on Indian History, Culture and Identity.* London: Penguin Books, 2005.

Chapter 5: Marketing in India

"Betting on the Big B," August 21, 2007, http://www.rediff.com/money/2007/aug/21ad.htm (last accessed December 1, 2007).

McKinsey Global Institute, "The Bird of Gold: The Rise of India's Consumer Market," May 2007, http://www.mckinsey.com/mgi/publications/india_consumer_market/index.asp (last accessed December 8, 2007).

Prahalad, C. K. *The Fortune at the Bottom of the Pyramid: Eradicating Poverty Through Profits.* Wharton School Publishing, 2005.

President Bush's quote on three hundred million middle-class Indians appears on http://fpc.state.gov/fpc/62503.htm (last accessed September 7, 2007).

Chapter 8: Traveling There and Living There

Kohls, L. Robert. *Survival Kit for Overseas Living.* London: Intercultural Press, 2001.

Paine, Jeffery. *Father India: How Encounters with an*

Ancient Culture Transformed the Modern West. New York: Harper Collins, 1998.

Singha, Sarina, et al. *Lonely Planet India.* Lonely Planet UK, 2006.

Conclusion

Bumiller, Elisabeth, *May You Be the Mother of a Hundred Sons.* New York: Ballantine Books, 1991.

Frater, Alexander. *Chasing the Monsoon.* New York: Owl Book Publishers, 1992.

INDEX

industrial designs, 173
Industrial Disputes Act, 174
Industrial Employment Act, 173
inflation, 23
infrastructure sector, 8-10
Intelenet Global Services, 142
Intellectual Property Appellate Board, 171
intellectual property laws, 169-73
International Trade Union Congress, 101
Internet service, 209
internships, 202-3
interpersonal distance, 73
Iran, 37
Islam (Muslims), 31-33, 67, 120
Israel, 7

Jaguar, 154
Jain, Indu, 36
Jain, Pradeep, 36
Jains, 36-37, 67
Jamnagar, 4
jet lag, 183-84
Jews (Judaism), 39
job retention, 94-96
Johnson & Johnson, 120
joint families, 164
joint ventures, 149-53, 169
Jones Lang LaSalle Meghraj, 14
Judas Thomas, 34
junior white-collar workers, 89-92

Kali, 29
Kamath, K.V., 108, 110-11
Kanbay, 153-54
Kapur, Anil, 127-28
karma, 30
Kashmir, 40
Khan, Shahrukh, 32
Khan, Ustad Amjad Ali, 59-60
Kingfisher, 187
kitchens, 207
Kleiner Perkins, 85, 140-41
knowledge-based services, 11-13
Kohlberg Kravis Roberts, 141-42
Kolkata (Calcutta), 43
Kudva, Vivek, 104-5, 149

Kumar, Arun, 49
Kumar, Rajesh, 76-77

labor. *See* human resources
lactose intolerance, 196
Land Rover, 154
language, 67-70, 81-82. *See also* English language
glossary of Indian English, 219-37
Larsen & Toubro, 144
law schools, 161
layoffs, 96-97
legal and accounting issues, 158-79
legal contracts, 162
Lenihan, Tim, 59, 62-63, 72, 78, 183, 195-96
Levi Strauss, 135
Lexus, 121
License Raj, xi-xiii, 22-23
liquor, 197-98
listed companies, 164-67
literacy rates, 88
living in India, 201-9
loans, 110-11
lobbying (lobbyists), 49
Lockheed Martin Corporation, 7

McDonald's, 26, 126
McGoldrick, Pat, 203
Maddison, Angus, 21-22
Madras Christian College, 86
Mahindra & Mahindra, 3, 95, 102, 104
Malhotra, Arjun, 13, 48-49, 57, 150
Malhotra, H. R., 171
Mammen, Vinoo, 34-35
managers, 79-82, 96-97
manners, 71-74
manufacturing sector, 2-5
Mao Zedong, 39
marketing, 103-36
four Ps of, 119-34
Indian seasons, 108-9
middle-class trends, 110-19
segments and trends, 105-8
youth in India, 134-35
Mauritius, 146-47
Maximum City (Mehta), 41-42

media, 10–11, 130–34
medical services, 198–200
medications, 193, 198–99
mega-trends, 1–16
Mehta, Suketu, 41–42
Mercedes, 121
mergers and acquisitions, 153–56
Merrill Lynch, 107
micro-financing, 111
middle class, 105–8
    trends, 110–19
midlevel employees, 92–93
Minimum Wages Act, 174
minorities, 191–92
Mittal, Laxmi, 109
mobile phones, 111, 115–16, 185–86
Modern Foods, 167
money, 137–39
Monster.com, 84
Morgan Stanley, 14–15
Moser Baer, 5
mosquitoes, 185, 193
Mphasis, 153
MRF Ltd., 34–35
MTV, 135
Mumbai, 40–42
Mumbai Airport, 9, 186
Murdoch, Rupert, 160
Muslims (Islam), 31–33, 67, 120

namaste, 72
names, 74–75
NASDAQ, 143–44
National Institute of Design, 86
National Stock Exchange, 142–44
National Thermal Power Corporation, 167
Naukri.com, 84, 141
Nayar, Sanjay, 99–100, 138–39, 145
Nazre, Ajit, 140–41
Neemix, 172
negotiations, 75–78
Nehru, Jawaharlal, 22
Nepal, 27
Nevis Network, 91–92
New Delhi, 43
News Corporation, 160

newspapers, 132–33
New York Stock Exchange, 143–44
Nichols, Bob, 190
Nicobar Islands, 6–7
Nooyi, Indra, 80
notice periods, 92
Novelis, 154
numerology, 66–67

Oberoi Construction, 15
OfficeTiger, 88–89, 94–95, 97, 153
Oil and Natural Gas Corporation (ONGC), 143, 166–67
Oracle, 153
Oster, Emily, 115
outsourcing (offshoring), 1, 11–13

Paine, Jeffery, 201
Pakistan, 32, 40, 184
Palmisano, Sam, viii–ix
palmistry, 66–67
Pant, Micky, 103, 126, 127, 131
Pantaloons, 125
parliamentary democracy, 45–46
Parsons Brinckerhoff (PB), 8–9
Parsvnath Developers, 36
partnerships, 163–64
Parvati (Durga), 29
passports, 184–85
Patel, Raj, 10–11
Patent Office, 171
patents, 152–53, 169–73
Patents Act, 171
Payment of Bonus Act, 174
Payment of Gratuity Act, 174–75
Payment of Wages Act, 173
Penguin India, 10–11
PepsiCo, 80, 122–23, 131
per-capita income, 25
performance-based pay, 94–95
physical contact, 73
Pinckney, William, 128–29
Pizza Hut, 126
place, 123–28
political parties, 46
polycultural society, 26–40
Prahalad, C. K., 107–8, 116

ABOUT THE AUTHOR

Gunjan Bagla is a management consultant who helps Western companies to succeed in India. His firm, Amritt (www.amritt.com), serves clients in the United States, Canada, and Western Europe in marketing to India, buying from India, and starting and running Indian operations. Amritt's clients include both large and emerging corporations in the West from a number of industries.

Bagla also teaches workshops and seminars for executives on how to become more successful in India, including a two-day seminar offered three times a year on the campus of the California Institute of Technology, Caltech. He writes and speaks on globalization and India frequently. His writing has appeared in *CIO Magazine, Daily Variety, Businessworld, Dataquest, India Journal,* and other publications. He publishes an electronic newsletter called *Globalization Is Great.*

Prior to starting Amritt, Bagla worked at both Indian and American companies with management responsibilities in marketing, sales, sourcing, manufacturing, and engineering. He was also a software entrepreneur.

Bagla earned a bachelor's degree in Mechanical Engineering at the Indian Institute of Technology Kanpur; he has an MBA with honors from Southern Illinois University–Edwardsville. He lives in Southern California with his wife, Smita, and two children, Avi and Anshika.

To learn more about Gunjan Bagla and Amritt Ventures, please visit www.amritt.com. If you have comments on the book, please e-mail info@amritt.com with the subject line "DBI-21 comment."